Lifting the Lid

A LIFE AT KINLOCH LODGE, SKYE

Claire
Macdonald

BIRLINN

For Godfrey

This edition first published in 2014 by
Birlinn Limited
West Newington House
10 Newington Road
Edinburgh
EH9 1QS

www.birlinn.co.uk

ISBN: 978 1 78027 213 9

British Library Cataloguing-in-Publication Data
A catalogue record for this book is available
from the British Library

Typeset by Mark Blackadder

Printed and bound by Grafica Veneta, Italy

Contents

Part Three: Our Third Decade, 1993–2003   131

Recipes

Part Four: Our Fourth Decade, 2002–2012   187

Recipes

Acknowledgements

Above everyone, I am completely indebted to Richenda Miers for her wise advice and skilful editing. But I am also grateful to many others – my daughter Isabella comes a close second to Richenda for her input into the book. I'm grateful to each of my other children for their great support and for their – usually – constructive criticism. It was my eldest daughter, Alexandra, who came up with the title of the book, so grateful thanks to her. Thinking up the title was one of the most difficult parts of writing it. My sons-in-law too have also had their input here, so thank you to Philipp, Tom and Peter!

I am also so grateful to all at Birlinn. It is such a leap of faith taking on a new author, and I hope I do them the credit they deserve. They produce beautiful books on such a wide variety of subjects, and I feel privileged that my book appears on their list.

My brother-in-law and agent, Jeremy Westwood, works hard both for me and with me, and I owe him a thank you for all his efforts. I also owe much to the advice, always worth taking, of my sisters, Milla and Liv.

My friends are so highly valued by me, and they contribute more than they could ever realize to my life. Minty and Gavin, Judith and Paul, Mary and John, Jane and Charlie, Lucy and John, Colin and April, Henrietta, Amanda, and Bridgie all count for so much; so too do many others. I could fill a whole page with their names, so I must stop here.

Lastly, without my darling Gog, *Lifting the Lid* simply wouldn't exist. We are, and always have been, in it together.

Preface to the Paperback Edition

———

Life never stands still. I finished writing *Lifting the Lid* towards the end of 2011 and much has changed since then. To start with, we succeeded in beginning and completing extensive alterations to Kinloch over a brief few weeks following the departure of our guests after New Year 2012/2013, and miraculously were ready to re-open as planned on 8 March 2013. These alterations encompassed installing a biomass boiler and re-plumbing both Kinloch lodges (central heating in the North Lodge has made the corridors and landings positively balmy!), extending the kitchen by two-thirds and refitting it with all manner of equipment, and re-doing all the bathrooms. We also made six suites and converted some rooms for staff accommodation. To have achieved all this within such a short space of time must be a record for construction anywhere in the British Isles, and all our wonderful team were local.

Tom has left Kinloch – he and Isabella are no longer together. Isabella now runs Kinloch, ably assisted by Marcello and his wife Claire, and Rachel MacKinnon. We were overjoyed to have retained our Michelin star again, for the fifth year running. And we have just broken all our previous records with our numbers of guests, both staying and coming to eat at Kinloch. We are thrilled!

Claire Macdonald, January 2014

Preface

On the last Friday of February 2011, my husband Godfrey and I set off from our home at Bellevue, on the Black Isle, to spend a couple of nights at Kinloch Lodge, the hotel on the Isle of Skye where we'd lived and worked for four decades, as we had cooking demonstrations on the Saturday and Sunday. We arrived to see a full car park and, inside, a happy party of eight local 'girls' (my age) was celebrating a special birthday with champagne teas. The whole place was alive with lights and, in an atmosphere of peace, log fires were burning brightly and the warm, friendly staff were attending to the needs of all the guests, both residents and those in for tea.

That evening Godfrey and I were joined by Araminta Dallmeyer – known as Minty, she is my greatest friend and my accomplice at nearly all my cooking dems. The three of us had dinner in Kinloch's dining room. As we looked around, we saw the dining room was full, every table taken. We had a most delicious dinner featuring local mussels, home-cured salmon, cod and scallops and the best beef, and the other guests seemed just as content with what they were eating. Wine flights – different wines to accompany the various courses – were being served to several of our fellow diners.

As well as the residents having lunch, a party of nine guests had booked for the lunch that would follow the Saturday morning dem. Each one chose chef Marcello's tasting menu and they didn't leave until about 4.30 in the afternoon. Sunday was similarly busy, with fourteen of the residents attending the cooking dems. Not all the Kinloch guests do come to the dems and we never quite know who is and who isn't staying for them.

Guests can choose to walk, snooze by one of our three log fires, relax and generally recharge their batteries for their busy lives. They eat some of Scotland's finest food and drink from one of the best wine lists in country and, if they like, they can sample an intriguing and wide selection of whiskies and beers produced all over mainland Scotland and its islands.

I found it simply amazing to be so busy at Kinloch at the end of February. Not that long ago, we wouldn't even have been open in March, let alone February, as people never used to contemplate taking a holiday in Highland Scotland in wintertime. But Godfrey and I had always worked towards Kinloch being open all year and, through one or two determined efforts to attract guests during the winter months, we have proved it to be not only possible but successful.

How it all began . . .

Introduction

About Us

Godfrey and I had very different upbringings. We are similar in that we are both one of three siblings. Godfrey is the second child and eldest son of Alexander – he was always known as Alasdair, the Gaelic form of Alexander – and Anne Macdonald, with an older sister, Janet, and a younger brother, Archie. I am the eldest child of Tommy and Jean Catlow, with two younger sisters, Camilla and Olivia. But there ends any similarity.

Godfrey was born in Ostaig House, on the southern peninsula of the Isle of Skye, where he lived and grew up. Like our own four children some decades later, he started his schooling at the local primary school at Ferindonald in Sleat but he was soon sent away to board at the Grange Home School in Edinburgh because he was deemed to be too much for his mother to cope with during his father's frequent absences from home, when he was Grand Master Mason of Scotland. By all accounts quite a handful as a small child, he was adventurous and exploratory but I suspect that the catalyst for his dispatch to a boarding school came when, aged six, he removed some lead from part of a roof, built a fire and melted it – ingenious for one so young but daunting for anyone trying to deal with him.

His childhood and teenage years were mostly spent out of doors, absorbing everything the seasons brought and fishing for anything, whether in the sea or the lochs. He was – and still is – fascinated by and extremely knowledgeable about butterflies and, although he is colour blind, it has never once occurred to me to question his unerring instinct for that which is edible when it comes to his passion for collecting fungi. And there is a profusion of different mushrooms and fungi, just for the picking, in the woods around Ostaig and even more in the woods around Kinloch. With no first cousins, his growing up was not terribly sociable at home and evolved around his numerous school friends. After the Grange Home School, he went to Belhaven Hill, at Dunbar, when he was eight and, from there, to Eton. He loved being at both but, equally, loved coming home at the end of each term to pick up on his numerous pursuits on his beloved island of Skye.

My growing up was completely different. My father was in the Royal Navy and we were lucky for two reasons. Unlike many service families, we had a permanent home in the north-west of England, in a large flat in my grandmother's house, Thurland Castle, in the Lune Valley in Cumbria. We also lived in all the fascinating places to which my father was posted, notably Malta; Virginia, USA; Rome, where he was naval attaché and Scotland. In between the foreign postings, we lived at home in Cumbria, with lots of friends around and frequent visits from our cousins. I am one of 15 first cousins and we are all extremely close, to this day. Wherever we lived overseas, my mother integrated us as a family – no shopping in the NAAFI for us. She immersed us in the local life of wherever we were lucky enough to be and we acclimatised accordingly. When we went to live in Virginia Beach, Liv, my youngest sister, then aged five, had not long started at the village school in Tunstall, Lancashire. She soon found friends to play with around our house and, within weeks, she was speaking in a most peculiar way – a combination of her own Lancashire accent crossed with that of her best friend who was from South Carolina.

My mother was much cleverer than any of her three daughters. During the Christmas and Easter holidays of the precious two years when we lived in Rome, she organised frequent excursions to archaeological sites, churches, art galleries and museums. I was fortunate to be old enough to absorb and appreciate all the wonders she unveiled for our education. Milla, my middle sister, was as receptive as I was, but I sometimes wonder how Liv managed – on a diet of regular stops for Coca-Cola and doughnuts, according to family lore. What a legacy our mother gave us during that time. It would last all our lives and be nurtured and built upon with future visits.

Marriage

Godfrey's father died, aged sixty-one, in November 1970. But his demise and the dreadful illness which preceded it were completely unimagined when Godfrey and I met in the Queen's Bar on Frederick Street, Edinburgh. I was on my way to a dance in the north of Scotland with someone else. Godfrey was apprenticed to the firm of Graham, Smart and Annan, Chartered Accountants, in Charlotte Square. We were introduced by an old friend of mine, Graham Beck, with whom Godfrey shared a flat. We were both nineteen years old and our romance began then. Godfrey and Graham used to drive to the Lune Valley in Godfrey's old Rover, known as Lars Porsena, which drank petrol at 12 miles to the gallon. They would invite themselves to stay for weekends and then Godfrey began to come on his own.

My first visit to Skye is the stuff of family legend because Godfrey had omitted to tell his parents that he was bringing me home. They rarely had anyone to stay, apart from Godfrey's school friends, and, unbeknownst to me, they had just endured the upheaval of having central heating installed. It was only as we drove down the drive to Ostaig that Godfrey casually told me that he hadn't informed them I would be with him. When we arrived, after what seemed to me to have been an interminable journey, all in the dark, their faces fell visibly. Later, I discovered that he had telephoned them from Edinburgh to say he was bringing me and had received a telegram requesting that he 'come alone or not at all'. To say that my welcome was muted is a major understatement. I had been brought up to make an effort socially and I certainly made one then.

On that first morning, I went down to breakfast to find Godfrey spluttering alarmingly and, within a few hours, everyone realised that flu had struck, resulting in us staying there for two whole weeks – my poor in-laws-to-be. However, we seemed to get along all right, though I was never entirely sure. It was on the way back to Edinburgh following this visit that Godfrey asked me to marry him. By this time we had both reached the great age of twenty, I being three months younger than him, and naturally we felt entirely grown-up. It never occurred to me to say anything other than yes, of course I would marry him. It felt right.

Asking permission to marry me was not entirely plain sailing. My father was, by then, becoming increasingly deaf following an evening at a dance given by friends, where the music was so loud that it triggered off a latent deafness caused during the Yangtse crisis in 1949, when the destroyer HMS *London*, on which he was serving, was hit by a torpedo. The ammunition had exploded quite close to him, mercifully not close enough to kill him but it affected his hearing two decades later. So, when Godfrey accompanied him down to the river, plucked up enough courage to say his bit about wanting to marry me and waited with baited breath for my father's response, all he got was: 'What was that? Were you asking me something?' He had to start all over again, speaking so loudly that startled cows looked up from their grazing nearby.

Although there was no question of anyone objecting, there was a certain amount of muttering about how young we were. However, we became officially engaged and were married six months later, on 14 June 1969, in our village church of St John the Baptist, Tunstall. Thurland Castle, my old home, had been sold the previous year and my parents had moved to a much more manageable house in the village. But we were still able to hold the reception at Thurland, as it was kindly lent back to us for the day.

Godfrey had never been south of Slough in his life. As a wedding present, his father offered us a tour of the Outer Isles, which we declined, and instead spent our honeymoon on the Amalfi Coast. As we drove away from the reception, Godfrey's father's last words were 'Don't drink the water'! Happily, Godfrey took to Italy like the proverbial duck to water. He loved the heat, the food and the drink, and we had a wonderful two weeks.

At the end of our honeymoon, we couldn't wait to get back to Edinburgh to start living in the flat we had bought in Lennox

Street, which I had been painting with a lot of help from my sister Milla. It was thrilling unpacking our wedding presents and starting our lives together. There were three in our marriage because one of our most precious wedding presents, given to us by Milla, was a tricolour Cavalier King Charles puppy called Lucy, a dog of great character who initiated the precedent for all the dogs we have subsequently owned – Ruler of the Roost.

Lucy, Godfrey and I went everywhere together. Like most of our dogs have been, she was very greedy. On one occasion, left in our Mini for a couple of hours, she ate a large box of fruit gums – the result was intriguingly gelatinous. Walks in the Dean Gardens were punctuated by stops to greet and be greeted by people whose dogs were friends. Early on in our married life with Lucy, when she was still slim enough, we would walk up our street early in the morning and she would slip through the railings of the Dean Gardens, potter about and do what she needed to do and then return to whichever of us was waiting on the pavement.

Married Life – of a Sort

None of us had realised that the cold my father-in-law was suffering from at our wedding and which continued through the following weeks was, in fact, throat cancer. But he had known. We discovered some months later that he had been advised to have an operation to remove his larynx, which he had declined, finding the prospect of being unable to speak impossible to contemplate. His life was one of public service. He sat on endless committees, one being the newly formed Hydro Board. His decision to opt for a delaying form of treatment, radiation, was therefore understandable.

We had only been in our new home for a couple of months when my father-in-law revealed the diagnosis and that he must undergo a course of three months' treatment in the Western General Hospital, in Edinburgh, very close to our flat. He had to spend from Monday to Friday in hospital and stayed with us each weekend, and my mother-in-law came to stay with us for the three months.

As his treatment progressed, my father-in-law (I never managed to call him Alasdair) suffered cruelly and bravely. The throat is the connection between the head and the rest of the body, and swallowing is vital, but his poor throat was burnt by the radiation. I became adept at making soft foods – soups, caramel custards, dishes he could swallow with little effort but nutritious enough to sustain him. Hospital food in those days was dire. On one occasion, when presented with the menu and seeing nothing possible for someone in his physical condition – pork pie with pickled beetroot was on offer among other things, which would have been like eating shards of glass in acid – he sent for the head of catering. Unfortunately, this man turned out to have been sacked some two months previously by the Highland Health Board or its then equivalent, on which my father-in-law sat.

It was not easy having my mother-in-law to stay for such a protracted length of time. She wasn't used to being away from her own home and I was new to their family and young. For her, it must have been strange not only being so far from all that was familiar to her but also being in a city. Although it was our home, it hadn't been for very long and neither Godfrey nor I felt very much in charge, so it was quite easy to be told what to do and how to do it, which I often bitterly resented later. Added to this, for the first couple of months after our marriage, we had loved having friends for supper and going to them, but now we felt we couldn't lead that sort of social life. And, underlying each day for everyone was, of course, the anxiety of what lay ahead for my father-in-law.

When the treatment ended, they went back to Ostaig and we picked up our lives again. Callous though it now feels even writing this, we had a lot of fun. We went to the north-west coast of Sardinia that summer of 1970 and spent two happy weeks in a villa with my parents, sisters and friends.

The day after we got back to Edinburgh the telephone rang

and we were summoned to Skye urgently – my father-in-law was terribly ill. We sped north. The old family doctor, Dr Campbell, had retired and we found a new GP was in charge. He overrode the decision of the doctor to keep my father-in-law in the island's Broadford Hospital where they had taken him. The new man called an ambulance to take him to Inverness for treatment from an ear, nose and throat specialist. This decision was made with the best will in the world and we were grateful but, with hindsight, keeping him in Broadford would have been kinder.

It was a Sunday, so there were no ferries except in emergencies, which this was. We raced off to Inverness, following the ambulance. At the hospital, my father-in-law stopped breathing as he was laid on the stretcher. He was resuscitated and had an emergency tracheotomy operation, with a tube in his throat to enable him to breathe. He was then sent home, where he lived for another three months – cruel months of increasing pain, suffering and misery.

I became extremely fond of my father-in-law despite his attitude towards Godfrey, his son and heir. Theirs had never been an easy relationship, with my father-in-law always expecting more of Godfrey and never able to praise anything he did. Yet, during those three months, it was Godfrey who nursed his father with the utmost gentleness and compassion.

We moved up to Ostaig because nursing him was far too much for one person and my poor mother-in-law was isolated. The tracheotomy tube had to be removed, sterilised by boiling and replaced twice a day. My father-in-law couldn't swallow and was fed by a feeding tube, and he bitterly resented the intrusions on his privacy. It was a frightening time. Initially we had the support of the district nurse and, during this early time, we went down to stay with my parents for a few days. While we were there, I had an emergency appendectomy – fate indeed. Godfrey went back to Skye without me, while I stayed with my parents to recuperate. When I was strong enough, I rejoined him, only to discover things had gone downhill dramatically.

My father-in-law, in an understandable rage, had told the district nurse never to come back following a tracheotomy change one morning when she had inadvertently hurt him. I am tempted to write down what he actually said to her but, understandable as it was under the circumstances, it wouldn't be fair to his memory. We had oxygen cylinders to hand and, on one terrifying occasion, I was left alone to sit with him while Godfrey drove his mother to Broadford to do her shopping. To my horror, he lit a cigarette and then fell asleep. I managed to remove the cigarette and stub it out, expecting a spectacular explosion to take both him and me into the next world as a result of the adjacent oxygen – it would have been a mercy for him but not for me. Poor man, it was such a degrading finale to his life.

*   *   *

One Sunday morning I was in our bedroom while Godfrey was next door changing the tracheotomy tube as my father-in-law sat in front of the dressing table. The radio in our room was playing Neil Diamond's 'Cracklin' Rosie' when Godfrey called me. His voice was controlled but urgent. I rushed in to see my father-in-law looking at himself in the mirror, blood gushing from the hole in his throat. I grabbed towels from the nearby bathroom. Mercifully he quickly lost consciousness and died within minutes. Thus the life of that fine, distinguished man ended in the house in which he had been born.

Because his demise had been so sudden and unexpected – he was only 61 – he had made no plans for his inheritance apart from appointing the family lawyer and the family accountant as his trustees. After his death, it rapidly became obvious that the desire of both these men was to discharge their duties as fast as they could and that the welfare of the family was secondary to this duty, which transpired to be a need to get rid of all debt. This was when we discovered to our horror that we had inherited not only a new set of death duties but a large part of the death duties inherited by my father-in-law on the death of his grandfather, and, the day after his death, we learnt that a loan from the Church of Scotland taken out the previous century had been called in. This loan had been for rebuilding the central part of Armadale Castle, which had burnt down in the mid-1860s and was now a ruin.

Godfrey also inherited the title Lord Macdonald, Macdonald of Macdonald, and, what matters to him above all else, the High Chiefship of Clan Donald, the largest of all the Highland clans. He is the 35th High Chief and the 8th Lord, but the two titles are unrelated.

Without consulting the family, the trustees decided that the whole estate, including Ostaig, the family house, must be sold with the minimum of delay and that, if things went really well, a small cottage might be retained for my mother-in-law, then in her mid 50s, and her son Archie, then aged fifteen and still at school.

We seemed to be living in a weird dream. The sums being discussed were like Monopoly money and Godfrey and I felt completely bewildered. If they are lucky, most newly married couples take on a mortgage. We had landed such a load of debt that perhaps it was lucky we felt it to be unreal. On the plus side – and, most importantly – we had each other. Just as well we had married young, we agreed, with a lifetime ahead to tackle whatever lay before us.

It was around this time that I developed a deep contempt for some lawyers – *some*, I stress. There are a few for whom I have great affection and respect but, alas, we didn't know them back then when we so badly needed wise advice. The saying that more Highland estates have been ruined by Edinburgh lawyers than for any other reason is well founded. I can't remember who said this originally, but I wish it had been me and I endorse it utterly.

Development – of the Inheritance

When the potential sale of the Macdonald estates became public knowledge, Godfrey was approached by a number of clansmen, among them Donald J. Macdonald of Castleton, the much-loved and respected clan historian. They were all anxious to form a charitable trust to buy the lands, the estate being considered of vital importance to Clan Donald as the last remaining land of the once mighty Kingdom of the Isles. The worldwide membership of Clan Donald was estimated to be in the region of ten million people and a fund-raising tour was planned by a committee of Macdonalds.

We were swept along on a wave of enthusiasm and, thus, the Clan Donald Lands Trust (CDLT) came into being. Oh, for the benefit of hindsight! If I was asked now whether I would do everything that we did for the CDLT again, I wouldn't hesitate to say 'Not in a million years!' Setting it up and fund-raising for it were surely two of our worst mistakes, and it has brought us nothing but angst. But the CDLT has to be seen as completely separate from Clan Donald worldwide.

Godfrey and I departed on 21 May 1971 for a three-month fund-raising tour of the United States and Canada. We met a vast number of people as we criss-crossed this continent and met with so much kindness wherever we briefed people about the project, which was an entirely new concept – that a clan should acquire its own lands. During this time, Godfrey suspended his chartered accountancy apprenticeship and, also during this time, he was elected the youngest member of Inverness County Council.

As a result of our North American trip, we had collected donations and pledges which, together with a commitment from the Royal Bank of Scotland, were enough to enable the Clan, in 1971, to outbid the highest contender for the Macdonald estates. This offer satisfied the trustees and provided enough finance for them to discharge their immediate burdens on the estate, allow the family to remain at Ostaig House and keep other small pockets of the estate. These included four run-down houses which my father-in-law had turned into hotels in the mid-1950s. They were the Ardvasar Hotel, the Isle Ornsay Hotel, the Duisdale Hotel and Kinloch Lodge. They were hotels in name only – the condition of the buildings, not to mention the standard of service offered, were remarkable for all the wrong reasons.

We decided to sell the Isle Ornsay Hotel and, after it was sold, we appointed a general manager, George Watson, whose remit was to oversee the remaining three hotels and improve standards as best he could within strict financial parameters. We returned to Edinburgh, where Godfrey resumed his apprenticeship and I started a small catering business, learning as I went along – which seems to have been the story of my life.

Sadly, George proved to be hopelessly out of his depth and, to add to his problems, he developed a severe illness which forced him to retire. And then, on Good Friday 1972, Ardvasar Hotel burnt down. It now became abundantly clear to us that we had no options – we must move to Skye and run the hotels ourselves.

We decided to move to the former head gardener's cottage up the hill behind Armadale. There was much to be done, not least to modernise the cottage. By now, we weren't only three in the family, including Lucy our dog. Our first daughter, Alexandra, was born in August that year.

Part One

Our First Decade
1973–1983

Moving to Skye

There was a slight complication in the weeks before our move from Edinburgh to Skye because Godfrey was to be guest speaker in Winnipeg for their St Andrew's Day celebrations that year. My stalwart parents agreed to look after two-month-old Alexandra and Lucy our dog while we nipped across to Canada. We were immensely grateful, then and subsequently: abandoning a precious baby is only thinkable if one is lucky enough to have trusted parents.

As with all our visits abroad for the Clan or for St Andrew or Caledonian societies, wherever we go we are fascinated. We have always felt incredibly lucky to be invited to visit such a variety of places, despite the agonising over what to wear – on my part, anyway. Winnipeg was very, very cold, but it was a dry cold and my other memory is that their St Andrew's Society seemed to consist entirely of ex-pat Scottish doctors. On our return, my parents met us at Prestwick, then the international airport for Scotland, with Alexandra and Lucy. We returned to Edinburgh briefly, packed up and moved north.

My mother, well experienced as a naval wife in moving house, had taught me how to assess the size of furniture and plan where things would fit in the next house. I applied this knowledge to our possessions, many of which had to go into storage in Skye because our new home was small. We loved it and were soon settled into a completely new way of life, though I must admit, I did miss my friends. I suppose my sense of isolation was partly due to Alexandra. I had left a life in Edinburgh where several close friends had had babies around the same time, where we were always in touch, comparing notes, and there were regular clinics to monitor the progress of our babies. In Skye, there was none of that then and I had no friends in those early days.

Before too long, however, three couples came into my life, bringing me fun and giving me their time and a sense of security. They were Clodagh MacKenzie and her husband, Colin, in their beautiful house at Kyleakin, Caroline and Charles Stewart, in Dunvegan, and Elizabeth and Jumbo Wakefield, at Carbost. All three couples were retired and had lived fascinating lives. They were kindness itself to me, Godfrey and little Alexandra. I've always hoped I was able to convey to them what a difference they made to me during my first years in Skye and subsequently. Then there were Jock and Evelyn Macdonald, at Viewfield in Portree, who were hospitable indeed, always inviting us for lunch whenever my parents came to stay. We loved going to Viewfield and I am so glad that our two eldest, Alexandra and Isabella, remember it with its walls filled with stuffed birds and the owl who gave me such a fright the first time I saw it blink – the only live bird in the house. And Godfrey's 'cousin' Sheila and her husband General Harry were also kind to us and we grew to love them.

Godfrey's Great Aunt Iona, who had lived in Portree House until her death just before we moved up, was a remarkable character and I loved her too. We gave our third daughter, Meriel, Iona as her second name. She and her mother had been in Berlin at the outbreak of the First World War, during which she lost her remaining three brothers, having lost the other during the Boer War. She had a keen sense of humour and I loved listening to her reminiscences. She was a hardy soul; her house was so cold that it was usually warmer going back outside.

Shopping took considerable adjustment. Everything remotely out of the ordinary had to be put on a lengthy list for our infrequent visits to Edinburgh. There was a travelling van run by Bruce Munlochy, who came once a month to our door, his van crammed with every sort of garment one could possibly need. In those days before disposable nappies, of which I strongly disapprove, I bought endless nappies and rubber knickers and all the necessities for our children and much else besides. Bruce – actually he was Sinclair Bruce, from Munlochy, on the Black Isle – always timed his visits to Sleat to coincide with the Masonic meetings. Kinloch was the consecrated meeting place for Lodge Macdonald of Sleat, founded by Godfrey's father in 1926. When we started running Kinloch as a hotel, the Masonic meetings posed a problem because reservations had to be taken around those dates. In 1983, they moved the meeting place for the Lodge to the Stables at Armadale Castle, making things easier for us.

When the birth of our second child was on the horizon, it was decided that we should swap houses with my mother-in-law and this entailed some necessary building in both houses. Gardener's Cottage became Armadale House, with more bedrooms and another bathroom added and a good kitchen. Ostaig turned out to have been standing on a wing and a prayer. The joist supporting the entire first floor was found to be rotten, so we had to do rather more than we had anticipated. Standing above the sea, it's a lovely house and we were happy there.

From the moment we arrived in Skye, our days were action packed as we tackled all the work needed to run Kinloch as a hotel, in line with new building requirements as well as necessary modernisation.

Kinloch Lodge and Our Aims as Hoteliers

Kinloch Lodge, built as a farmhouse in the mid-1600s, was extended in 1850, to become one of several shooting lodges built on the Macdonald estates at that time, during a brief spell of affluence, due to the then thriving kelp (seaweed) market. By the time my father-in-law inherited from his grandfather, in 1947, Kinloch was one of a number of rapidly deteriorating buildings on the estate, long before such houses were in demand as second homes. In those days no one wanted to buy a run-down house in the Highlands without plenty of land attached for sporting use.

On the advice of one of his friends during a visit to the New Club in Edinburgh, my father-in-law instructed his factor to turn Kinloch into a hotel. 'Very good, my Lord,' said Mr Simpson and, thus, in 1952, began the rebirth of a semi-crumbling building.

Kinloch had no electricity in those days – nor did Ostaig, for that matter – and Godfrey remembers well its installation that same year. Raw sewage from the house flowed directly into the sea at the bottom of the garden. The water supply came from a mile up the hill behind, through a pipe buried just below the surface, which, as a result, froze during any prolonged frosty spell. There were fifteen bedrooms, served by three bathrooms, and the only heating came from two log fires. The cooking was done on an old anthracite range which also heated the water. My father-in-law had been persuaded to build on a modest extension to provide a larger dining room, with extra bedrooms upstairs, which was when the number of bedrooms was brought up to fifteen. The whole job cost £800.

In its first year, Kinloch turned over just under £1,000 and the wages were £300. Open for four months of the year, it had an occupancy rate of 20 per cent. Over the next 20 years Kinloch staggered on and certainly never made much impression on the increasing volume and importance of the tourist industry to the fragile Highland economy. My father-in-law, through his factor, who might have understood the value of cattle and sheep at market but had no understanding of the value of a two-legged tourist, employed a succession of managers to run Kinloch. The majority of these were alcoholics or crooks or, in some cases, both.

The installation of electricity, an Aga in the kitchen and an oil-fired boiler for hot water made no difference to the continuation of a loss-making business. The accounts for 1970 show a gross loss, with the purchase of food and drink exceeding the total turnover.

This was the Kinloch Lodge that Godfrey and I inherited. We went up the Christmas before we decided to move permanently to run the hotels ourselves and spent New Year there. Apart from brave members of my family and great friends who joined us for the 'celebration', it was the most miserable five days imaginable. The tiny fire in the drawing room smoked copiously and gave out little heat. The curtains billowed in the draughts, even though the windows were shut. In the bedroom we occupied over those few days, the double bed was pushed up against the wall, which meant that I had to clamber over Godfrey if I wanted to get out of bed earlier than he did. A stay in the most spartan of guest houses would have been like visiting the Ritz in comparison to those five days we endured at Kinloch so, when we decided, a few months after this, to move up and run it ourselves, I must admit the prospect was slightly daunting.

Our aim was to make Kinloch into the sort of hotel we would have wanted to stay in ourselves – one serving really good food, using local produce as much as possible and providing our guests with warmth, comfort and endless hot water. A true Highland welcome and good service came high on our list, too. It sounds fairly straightforward, but it turned out to be rather more complicated to achieve.

Builders

This book is supposed to be about Kinloch, but it is impossible to separate it from the other two major bits of building work we had underway at the same time, in Duisdale and Ardvasar hotels. If the burning down of Ardvasar had been traumatic for the village of Ardvasar for which it had been the central point, it was even more so for us. Although the middle section had burned to the ground, the bits on either side remained standing and, because the whole place wasn't razed to the ground, our insurance refused to pay out more than £27,000.

Because it was Grade 2 listed, everyone had carte blanche to apply maximum bureaucracy to the rebuilding and the builders had an excuse to add rows and rows of noughts to the costs. New fire regulations were responsible for the work required in Duisdale Hotel, as well as for a lot of the work necessary for Kinloch. These new regulations were the result of a devastating fire in a hotel in Oban the previous year, when ten people lost their lives. Until then, Kinloch had had no fire precautions apart from windows through which to jump and neither did any other Highland hotel. The strict fire safety programme that was subsequently introduced for all hotels was for the individual interpretation of the various local authorities, each of which, as we discovered late in the day, adopted a different approach. By law, a fire certificate had to be granted by May 1974 for any hotel to be allowed to function. The penalty for not doing so was to be closed down.

The reconstruction plans, including fire precautions, for Ardvasar, Duisdale and Kinloch were drawn up and put out to tender. For various reasons, including rampant inflation in double figures and the glut of building work required by every other hotel racing to achieve fire certificates, no builder was prepared to come and work in the islands for a fixed price. The only way they would work was on a time-and-material basis, which was a recipe for a financial nightmare for us and the proverbial 'dripping roast' for the firm of builders from Elgin we employed. Preliminary estimates for the cost to rebuild Ardvasar were in the region of £150,000. The final cost was £400,000. By my reckoning, this puts Ardvasar Hotel and the Scottish Parliament at Holyrood on a similar footing, except that the purse providing these vast sums for Ardvasar belonged to us, whereas Holyrood was paid for out of the public purse – a monument to the vanity of those in charge. No one could ever think of Ardvasar as a monument to anything except gross expenditure.

Finding Our Feet

The first few weeks following our move from Edinburgh, in November 1973, went by in a haze. The building work at Kinloch was top priority – it was imperative that we got our Fire Certificate in time to open the following April.

Before we swapped houses with my mother-in-law, Godfrey spent most of his time driving from our home in the Gardener's Cottage up the hill behind Armadale to one or other of the hotels and I made daily visits to Kinloch with Alexandra in her carrycot on the back seat of the car. Kinloch was virtually gutted. The number of bedrooms was to be reduced from fifteen to twelve, with one of them on the ground floor for guests who couldn't manage stairs, and six having their own bathrooms – an almost unheard of luxury at that time. Our main problem was that all the work was virtually unsupervised by the Elgin-based architect, who felt unwilling to be involved as there was no enforceable contract. I went round the house, not really having a clue about anything, picking my way through the chaos of ripped up floorboards, with baths and basins stacked against the walls of corridors both upstairs and down. Looking at the sea of rubble everywhere – both indoors and covering a large amount of lawn outside – it seemed impossible to believe that order would ever be achieved, let alone a calm, clean house suitable for paying guests, but optimism reigned supreme.

*   *   *

We had a small hitch before Christmas. On 17 December, on his way to Kinloch in our Mini, Godfrey skidded on black ice and hit the approaching bus head-on. The driver leapt from the bus and said, 'My God, I've killed the Lord!' which, mercifully, he hadn't. But the Lord did sustain severe injuries to his left knee. He was taken to the excellent hospital in Broadford, assessed by the then surgeon, John Ball, and his leg duly plastered from groin to toe. (Unfortunately years of trouble followed until the knee joint was replaced thirty-five years later.) He had to stay in hospital for some weeks and it was during this time that he sustained another injury – this one completely self-inflicted. He was then a smoker and one evening, having been given his painkillers and a cup of tea, talked the night sister into letting him smoke. He fell asleep and woke the next morning with a third-degree burn on his finger, the cigarette having burnt right through to the bone – he was extremely lucky that he hadn't burnt the hospital down at the same time. John Ball had the last laugh – his skilful skin graft took skin from the inside of Godfrey's arm, which meant that using crutches was impossible until the arm had healed.

My saintly parents drove to Skye to spend Christmas and New Year in the cottage with me and Alexandra, but their car broke down on the way and they had to hire another. My mother said that the faces of the car-hire people were a vision, as she and my father unpacked their car and packed into the hired car all the Christmas presents they were bringing north, as well as a dead hare and several pheasants.

When Godfrey was released from hospital, he quickly mastered getting upstairs on his bottom. He was very frustrated by his inability to get around on crutches and my parents and I took it in turns to drive him to Kinloch. Somehow we got through those interminable weeks until March when, to everyone's huge relief, the plaster was removed.

Meanwhile, the building work progressed and things gradually came together. Godfrey and I were completely unprepared for the amount of work required to finish and equip such a large building and prepare it for business as a hotel. More to the point, we had no idea how on earth we were to finance the refurnishing and refurbishing. Every single step needed decisions – and payment.

Salvation strode into our lives in the form of Bill Cowan. How we found him or he us I cannot remember, though how I could forget something that meant so much to us is a mystery. Bill, a chain-smoking Glaswegian, worked for a company called RoomService, which provided us with tables, chairs, beds, bedside tables, chests of drawers, crockery, cutlery – everything, in fact, that we needed, including signs for the top of the road. And, best of all, everything we got through them could be paid for over several years. Financial salvation!

From then on, we had the advice and support of this wonderful man, who became a true friend. For a few days, my life became one of paper. I had to go through endless leaflets of different styles of furniture and all the time there was Bill Cowan at my elbow, advising on which were the best ones for us. He was invaluable and the quality of the furniture provided under his guidance by RoomService was such that now, forty years later, some of the chairs, re-covered several times since they first arrived, are still in use.

A Hiccup . . . and the Launch of Kinloch Lodge

During February 1974, with our April deadline for opening fast approaching, we struck a hitch. The required emergency lighting system necessary for the Fire Certificate had been installed by a firm of electricians from Glasgow but, to our horror, it transpired that the regulations according to the Glasgow Fire Authority were not the same as those of the Inverness County Fire Authority.

We had no choice. Intractability on the part of those responsible for granting the Fire Certificate meant that all the newly laid carpets throughout the corridors had to come up, and then the floorboards. It seemed incredibly stupid to me and still does all these years later because, either way, electrics done according to the Glasgow regulations still meant lives saved in the event of a fire. But my protestations were in vain and all the new wiring had to be redone, as did the estimates for the final cost, yet again.

All this time, we were competing against the clock. We had become so bogged down in decisions and choosing furnishings, not to mention endless dealings with bureaucracy, that suddenly we realised with horror that we must turn our thoughts to staff for Kinloch and to the bookings. We had no book or reservation sheets for these and we entered the few bookings we had in a page-a-day diary.

That we were ready to open on 3 April was little short of

miraculous and involved the help of family and close friends. Godfrey's mother spent much of the two weeks beforehand on her hands and knees with a dustpan and brush; my sister Liv came up to look after Alexandra in exchange for us clearing off her overdraft; our friend Peter Leggate arrived and auctioned the old hotel furniture for which there was a surprising market; my parents helped by doing any and everything that needed to be done. We were amazingly lucky to have all those willing hands to help clean, hang pictures and generally clear up, both inside and out, after the builders had finally departed.

When we turned our thoughts to finding staff, word spread locally. One day we were approached by Millie MacLure, who came to ask us if we had a job for her. From the Isle of Lewis, she was married to Donnie, then a crofter from the nearby township of Drumfearn, and, during this frantic time, I got to know her really well. There is nothing like working beside someone else, cleaning public loos, both with our hands down the S bends, to accelerate friendship. Millie had done a lot more in her life than cross the Minch from Lewis to Skye. She had worked as an au pair in Germany and was eminently capable at just about every-thing and very soon I counted her as my best friend on Skye. She handled all the secretarial work and was excellent with people, both staff and guests. Her quiet dignity and calm serenity are just what's needed in any tricky situation and she is also an extremely good cook. For the next two decades, Millie played a major role in our lives and it broke our hearts when she told us, after twenty years of our shared life at Kinloch, that she and Donnie had decided to move to her home island of Lewis with their growing children, Margaret and Andrew.

We also took on a married couple to live in and to be in charge when we were away. Both were completely new to the hotel business – he had been a sub-postmaster in central Scotland and she had worked in their local library. Seeking adventure, they applied for a job with us. Well, they were certainly right in that respect but, in truth, their idea of helping to run a hotel was extremely wide of the mark. Mrs H. was supposed to help me cook and serve dinner. I should have smelled a rat when, at their interview and as I was waxing lyrical in my descriptions of the sort of food that we intended to give our guests, she said, 'Yes, we'll be needing to get in a good stock of Baxter's soups, then.' I thought she was joking, but she wasn't. They both seemed happy at the prospect of cooking breakfast, but as 3 April approached and I had yet to see Mrs H. roll up her sleeves and make anything at all in the kitchen, doubts crept into my mind. These doubts were confirmed on The Day, 3 April, when I was busy cooking dinner for our very first evening as hoteliers. I had nipped back to our house that afternoon to check on Alexandra, who was being looked after by Sheila MacPherson, a friend to this day. All was well and peaceful at home, Alexandra was happy with Sheila, so back I went to Kinloch to find Mrs H. having a bath. When she eventually appeared in the kitchen, she was all dressed up and seemed surprised when I offered her an apron. She told me that she was going to mingle with our guests, all six of them. I remember very little of Mr H. – probably just as well – and suffice to say that they had gone within the week. They were not missed.

Sheila, from Alness in Rossshire, was married to John MacPherson and they lived down towards the Point of Sleat. Their two daughters were contemporaries of our second and third daughters and would grow up and go to school together but that was in the future. We also employed two sweet girls, Linda and Pauline, who had answered an advert my mother had put in the *Lancaster Guardian*, one of our two local newspapers back in the Lune Valley. They quickly learnt under Millie's expert instruction and were hard working and a great asset.

Staff at Kinloch during Our First Year

Our first year was a harsh lesson in people management: we got through thirty-four members of staff in that time, a fact in which we take no pride. By the close of our first season, we were left with just Millie MacLure and Iain MacEachern. Iain could do anything and did it well. He started as the gardener at Kinloch but, following the departure of another couple, he came to work inside. The son of a crofter from Islay, he had served in the army as a commissioned officer and had a natural confidence with people. He had no experience whatsoever of the hospitality industry but then neither had we – we were all learning at the same time. Within a few weeks, he became an accomplished barman, housekeeper and cook.

The couple Iain took over from indoors had been a disaster. Engaged to be married, she was a good cook, he a complete twit who loved to regale the guests with endless tales of his sporting prowess. One day, to our horror, we saw him pick up a water jug, in mid conversational flow to several guests, take a great swig from it, wipe his mouth with the back of his hand, burp loudly and carry on recounting tales of his skills with a gun or rod. The facial expressions of the guests mirrored how we both felt – shock and disbelief. We learnt later that his water-jug-swigging was a frequent occurrence that we had missed on previous occasions. He was a hopeless boozer and the finale came with the arrival of her parents, appalled at their daughter's choice of fiancé. There was a very public row between the four of them, ending with them all driving away, out of our lives forever.

The date is engraved on my heart, 4 July, the anniversary of American Independence but far more relevant in our lives as the start of the Glasgow Trades Fair. This is the annual fortnight when Skye fills up with all those who come from the island but live and work in Glasgow and it's our busiest time, or used to be.

I de-veined sweetbreads that evening for the first time in my life – the departed fiancée-cook had put them on the menu, along with a more straightforward roast. I've never liked sweetbreads since that day – nothing to do with their taste, everything to do with association.

Early in our life at Kinloch, a sweet girl from West Linton, who had done Celtic Studies at Edinburgh University, came to help us. She met and married a young architect who had dropped out of architecture and was working as a gardener and living in a small house belonging to his employers, over at Ord. Alasdair and Jenny Alldridge came into our lives and have been a part of them ever since. Alasdair decided to use his architectural training and was offered a job with Wittet's, the Elgin architects who opened an office in Broadford, with him in charge. Jenny worked part-time in the kitchen at Kinloch, where, amongst many other things, she baked the best bread of any of us.

The trouble was that their house went with Alasdair's job at Ord, so leaving the job meant they were looking for somewhere to live. We offered them a potential site on the shore, at the bottom of the garden, warning them that they would always have hotel guests wandering around, as they sauntered down from Kinloch to walk along our shore. This didn't put Jenny and Alasdair off and they built themselves a house on the site of the old kennels, Jenny doing as much of the physical backbreaking work as Alasdair, and they employed Alec, who then lived at the Kinloch farm, to help with the really heavy work. Having moved in, they settled down to life within the Kinloch compound and subsequently, over several years, their three children were born, Ruth, Tommy and Jack. Our children became great friends, even though they were older, and Jenny was patience itself with each of them if they went down to play. As they grew older, Ruth, Tommy and Jack each worked at Kinloch after their schooldays were over. It was extremely handy for them to have part-time work a short walk away and extremely handy for us having them. Jenny is a great help to me, these days, in the preparation for our cooking dems at Kinloch. She is diligent and fits in preparation for demonstrations between her other work and commitments. We all get together for supper on a couple of occasions each year and, in between times, Jenny and I catch up and communicate via email.

Food

Food was – is – the most important thing in my life apart from Godfrey and our children. I am not a taught cook – I am learning all the time and maintain that I will go on learning till I draw my last breath, which I always hope will be following a good meal. All those years ago, I had a clear idea of the type of food I wanted to provide for our guests – dinner party-type cooking, using as much local produce as I could lay my hands on. Seasonal food was my aim, but it proved very difficult to source.

To start with, during the evenings in the run-up to our opening, I had got hold of a large, leather-bound ledger. With the *Cordon Bleu* food magazines, published weekly, to hand, I worked out fifteen days of possible menus and wrote out all the recipes involved. By no means every dish and recipe I recorded was from these magazines – many were my mother's and many were gleaned from years of copying down recipes from various publications. One tremendous source was the then *Times* cookery writer Katie Stewart. Her recipes were and still are invaluable – they don't date and I learnt a lot from them. One springs to mind above all others – the need to add lambs' liver to game soup. The liver gives a velvety texture and subtle flavour which people find impossible to put their finger on. If you leave it out, the loss to the soup is great.

Godfrey and I decided that a choice of two dishes for each of the three courses would be about right and could be handled by a kitchen staffed by cooks, with me at the helm, as opposed to one with a brigade of trained chefs. We also offered one soup between the first and main courses, with no choice. It seemed to me a shame to include soup as one of the two first courses because that cut back on the potential range of dishes we could offer.

I must admit that the photographs at the top of every recipe within those *Cordon Bleu* magazines were themselves one of my greatest sources of inspiration – those and my innate greed. I love food. I am fascinated by it – the taste of individual items, the combination of tastes and textures, too. Luckily, this fascination has stayed with me, so far, all my life. Back at the start of our lives running Kinloch, however, it was one thing to have ideals about all the foods I wanted to buy and another matter entirely to get them. The prime example was fruit and vegetables. Back in the early 1970s we had a fruit and veg delivery every two weeks during the season and the season was the five months from May to September. Most people opened their hotel or guest house or bed and breakfast at Easter and so during April we somehow got through with buying fruit and veg locally, which was incredibly difficult when it was often impossible to buy a tomato in a tin never mind a fresh one. I would plead and cajole – I even thought of trying threat but couldn't think of anything with which to threaten – begging the wholesalers to bring me fruit and veg beyond what they normally stocked – carrots, cabbage, potatoes, onions, oranges, lemons and that was about it. I wanted exotica like mushrooms, which were being farmed fifty-two weeks of the year, but I was told they were too perishable. I pleaded with them to deliver to us hoteliers before the shops, to cut back on any perishable potential, but my pleas fell on deaf ears.

After we swapped houses with my mother-in-law and moved into Ostaig House, we employed a gardener. He's dead now and shall be nameless – so friendless was he that there were only two people at his funeral. He was an odd man who wore a wig which was glued into place and during hot weather the glue tended to melt in a treacle-like trickle down the sides of his face. We tried, through his debatable horticultural skills, to grow the vegetables we wanted to give our guests. He planted a vast amount of carrots, against our instructions – one of the few vegetables we could get delivered – and even his carrots didn't succeed. He told us that they had a blight called 'clubfoot'. I was clueless in the garden and, truth to tell, I'm not much more knowledgeable now, though I love gardens, flowers, fruit and veg and am a fantastic weeder, so I believed everything he told me. Nothing he grew thrived. Hopes would be raised as things sprouted, only to be dashed, yet again, always due to circumstances beyond his control, usually a blight of odd name.

We had to rely on frozen vegetables to a far greater extent than ever I imagined would be necessary. I soon learnt that buying frozen puréed spinach was a complete waste of money as, when it thawed, we were left with a useless puddle of tasteless, suspiciously too-bright green sludge. However, frozen leaf spinach was my salvation for soups, roulades and a host of other recipes. I still make one of my favourite recipes of those days: spinach and garlic terrine, which we served with seeded and skinned tomatoes, sliced thinly, and vinaigrette dressed.

Frozen petits pois were another standby because so much could be done with them. I sliced back bacon very thinly and fried the strips with finely diced onions, then added the peas – delicious. I also braised lettuce and onions and mint with petits pois. We made soup with peas, onions and apples, sometimes using pears instead of apples, and I used puréed peas with mint stirred into a good béchamel sauce, to serve with roast rack of lamb together with a coarse tomato and garlic sauce – a good contrast, both of taste and texture. As for cabbage, well, I don't know where we would have been without cabbage. I often think back to those days and wish I had written a book called *Forty Ways to Cook a Cabbage*.

We were adventurous indeed with what vegetables we had, but there were no alternatives and I remember one day Millie and I even stuffed onions and baked them. We spent so much more time trying to make vegetables interesting than is ever needed in these days of choice and plenty. I think it was our second or third year when a new fruit and veg wholesaler – the Macleods based in Portree – started delivering to us and they were marvellous. For a start, they delivered weekly and years later this became twice weekly. They listened. They sought out produce I asked for and brought it – things like Seville oranges to make into marmalade. How I appreciated them. They were and still are extremely hard working – they are also the local undertakers for Skye and the neighbouring mainland, Lochalsh. To me, Norman and Donnie Macleod epitomise the quality of service and entrepreneurial spirit that can be found in a great many family businesses throughout Scotland.

More about Food

My determined aim was that everything eaten by our guests should be made using the Kinloch kitchen and, with considerable finesse, it was. Take bread, for instance. The only bread we could buy locally was the ubiquitous sliced white and I wanted our guests to have good bread, so there was nothing for it but to make it myself.

My abhorrence of the smell of fresh yeast goes back to when I was eight. My father was posted to Norfolk, Virginia, and off we all went on a Cunard liner for this new adventure. (I remember breakfasting each morning on the liner on strawberries, with French onion soup for my main course and Ovaltine as my chosen drink, eight mornings in a row and I also remember a man, returning to the States from a holiday in Europe, bought as a result of having won a quiz game, who ate steak and Stilton for breakfast.) My parents found a house in Virginia Beach, where we settled into our new life, but unfortunately I was suffering, unattractively and extremely painfully, from recurring boils. The local hospital diagnosed a blood disorder for which the treatment was a daily dose of yeast, the vile taste of which I shall never forget. (I also remember being mystified that then, in the 1950s, there were two entrances to the hospital and two waiting rooms – one for white people and one for black.) The remedy did the trick and cured my boils, leaving me with my lifelong loathing of fresh yeast. All those years later, when I rejoiced at getting my hands on the stuff, I found that I simply couldn't work with it, so repellent was its smell. Smell is taste, as you will know, with two exceptions. Only salt and citrus are tasted on our taste buds – everything else we eat is tasted through our sense of smell.

With recipe to hand, therefore, I embarked on my bread-making career using dried yeast. My bread improved on a daily basis and now I positively love making bread; there is something so satisfying about the whole process. It can't be hurried and nor, once baked, can the cooling process be rushed; trying to fast-cool bread in a draught, for example, results in tough bread. As with so many other things, patience is the key to good bread-making. As my confidence grew, so too did my experimenting with tastes and textures. We always made a basic bread using granary flour but we also made herb breads, cheese and mustard bread, roasted onion bread and, of course, hot cross buns at Easter and Stollen at Christmas, with a good layer of home-made marzipan wrapped in the fruity dough. I've always said that, had I been able to buy good bread, I would never have bothered to make it, being inherently lazy, but what a lot of pleasure I would have missed. I maintain also that, no matter how good the bread one can so easily buy these days is, with its varying flavours, it is always 'safely' seasoned. When you make your own, you can add as much taste and flavour as you like.

I also made small scones flavoured with chopped herbs and grated cheese for serving with our soup course. These proved to be useful split in half as the base for canapé-style toppings – a batch of predominantly dill-flavoured miniature scones, for example, with a smoked fish pâté on top or a parsley and chive scone with a slice of rare roast beef on a dollop of horseradish crème fraîche.

I learnt on a daily basis and I reckon that now, forty years on, I'm still learning. Millie learnt with me and so did Peter MacPherson.

Memorable Members of
Staff during Our First Decade

Early in our second year, Peter MacPherson, a young man from the nearby township of Camus Cross, where he was born and brought up, came to work at Kinloch for a few weeks. He was recruited for our nearby hotel, Duisdale, but it opened later in the year than we did so he came to Kinloch to give us a hand. He was actually trained in dining-room work but one day he made a sponge cake, light and delicious, so Millie and I got him into the kitchen, where he became a very good cook. That year, when it was time for him to return to Duisdale, it was hard to let him go, so the following year he came to work with us at Kinloch and there he remained for thirty-four mostly happy years, until he had to leave for personal reasons. I will always be grateful to him for all his kindnesses – not the least for putting a hot-water bottle into my bed the night we moved from Ostaig to make Kinloch our home, seemingly such a small thing but enormously appreciated. Many years later, when my father had a stroke just before all the family were due to come to Kinloch for Christmas, Peter stepped in to help me in the most invaluable way possible, giving practical help and support during such a difficult time, and he moved in to look after the dogs and hold the fort. He also packed up all the food we had prepared for a big family Christmas, ready for me to transport down to the Lune Valley, where we had managed to find part of a house big enough to fit us all in for the weeks my father was in hospital.

*　　　*　　　*

Angela – or Angelica, as we know her – came to work with us at Kinloch and I credit her as being the person above all others from whom I learnt so much about cooking. She hasn't changed from the day she arrived all those years ago and she is now married to John Pargeter with two grown-up children, Jessica and James.

Hailing from Devon, she is tall, pretty and blonde. An

excellent mimic and a brilliant cook, she always got on with Peter like a house on fire – but she got on with everyone. She came to Kinloch on and off because she was also highly valued and loved by everyone else for whom she cooked, dotted around Scotland. I always felt safe when she was in the kitchen. She seemed so much more competent than I ever felt and I only hope I have given her due credit in the introductions to several of my books. The dish that springs to mind when I think of Angelica is herb crêpes with smoked trout and cucumber filling. She cooked so many delicious dishes, both savoury and sweet, with such panache and so inspiring were her ideas that I caught on fast.

I credit myself with two successful attempts at matchmaking and Angelica and John are one. When they got married from Kinloch, it was a truly happy day, marred only for me because I had to leave the celebrations early to drive to Glasgow to fly to New York. I was to be guest speaker at the Wadsworth Atheneum Museum in Hartford, Connecticut, my chosen subject being the one with which I was becoming ever more familiar – 'Food in Scotland'.

Meanwhile, our reputation at Kinloch was slowly growing. We were included in the *Good Food Guide* and, within five years, Kinloch was awarded a Tureen, that coveted award for serving really good food, and we also got a write-up in the *Good Hotel Guide*.

As I've already mentioned, we tried our best to use locally grown wild foods, picking vast quantities of mushrooms, particularly chanterelles, which grow in abundance in the woods around Kinloch. On one memorable day during our first year, Godfrey went on a mushroom-picking expedition and came home with a staggering twenty-eight pounds of field mushrooms. I remember cooking them in as many different ways as I could think of, including an inky-dark mushroom soup, using one vast mush-room alone, which was so large that it overflowed the edges of a twelve-inch plate.

During our first few years, it was impossible to buy fresh

cream – the last dairy on Skye, at the Home Farm in Portree, had ceased to function (and is now an excellent care home for the elderly). We could buy frozen double cream, which came in small cylindrical shapes, each about 1 cm thick and 4 cm long. I always thought of it as a long tweak at a cow's udder, yielding double cream rather than rich milk. It seems impossible to imagine life without the easy access not only to cream but also to two types, double and single, as well as crème fraîche and all the different flavours of yoghurts that we now have from the shelves of our local Co-op.

The Tariff and Finance Generally

The purpose of running a hotel – or any business, for that matter – is to make a living and provide employment. Looking back, I see with amazement that, in our first year, a night in one of our best rooms, including breakfast, cost £5 per person and dinner was £1.75. It is worth noting that, in those distant days, VAT was only 10 per cent whereas now 20 per cent of all our guests' bills goes straight to the government in VAT. At the end of our first season, we turned over £23,000 and made a loss of £2,000.

Godfrey's training as a chartered account was a great help but, for him, it must have been a bit like being a doctor and feeling ill – our finances were a nightmare. We were not only running Kinloch but also rebuilding Ardvasar Hotel, installing the regulation fire precautions at Duisdale and adding more bathrooms at the same time. We still actually owned a fourth hotel then – Isle Ornsay or Eilean Iarmain, as it is now known – and this widened our financial net to include what was evolving from the Clan Donald Lands Trust.

Thanks to the fund-raising trip that Godfrey and I took in the year following his father's death and the worldwide appeal organised from the Edinburgh Society of Clan Donald, the trust had raised sufficient funds to buy most of the family estates but, by now, some two years later, it was having difficulty raising the balance of the money needed to pay for them. Godfrey was in the extremely difficult position of being Chairman of the Clan Donald Lands Trust as well as heir to his father's estates. It was decided to resell the northern half of the estates and a purchaser materialised in the form of Iain Noble, a 38-year-old merchant banker with family connections to Argyll.

Ian Noble made it a condition that he must be allowed to buy the small hotel at Isle Ornsay, which he intended to use as his base. Godfrey agreed and earmarked the proceeds of the sale to go towards the costs of the Kinloch refurbishment, but it took Noble three years to pay for the hotel, forcing us to enter into protracted negotiations with the Bank of Scotland to enable payment for the work being done on the other two hotels, Ardvasar and Duisdale. Banks were extremely reluctant to lend to seasonal businesses, particularly those with poor trading records, and there weren't many poorer than ours.

This proved to be the final straw for Godfrey's father's trustees. They promptly resigned, saying that the financial future of the family was too uncertain for them to be able to continue in office. My contempt for them was searing, particularly as they were supposed to be family friends as well as professionals. I didn't really understand the situation except that it left us without any form of financial adviser or guidance – not that they had ever been of any actual help – but I saw it as an abandonment of Godfrey and his family, leaving us to sink or swim, according to whatever fate held in store for us. This was not my idea of how friends should behave.

As the costs for the Ardvasar and Duisdale hotels continued to escalate, it became obvious that a large capital injection was the only answer, so we put Duisdale on the market. However, the sale wasn't completed till 1977 by which time, even with substantial help from the then Highlands and Islands Development Board, we had had to enter into what Godfrey refers to as 'a devil's partnership' with the Bank of Scotland.

The Public Bar

When we embarked on running Kinloch as a hotel, the room to the right of the front door on entering was a public bar. It's a pretty room with a fireplace and we kept a fire burning there and in the large drawing room for most of the year. Having a public bar was a mixed blessing. It was good because visitors came and enjoyed a drink or had one of the bar lunches we served during those early years, mostly consisting of leftover dishes from the preceding night. Our lunchtime guests were very well catered for – if I remember correctly, we charged just £1 a head. This plus side of the public bar boosted our cash flow but the minus side involved some of the locals. Kinloch is a mile off the main road which, in those days, was a single-track road with passing places and anyone coming just to drink had almost certainly been banned from the other, more accessible bars. It wasn't hard to spot trouble when it walked through the front door because it was so well dressed. For men of that era, who had been through National Service, it was essential to be smartly turned out before going out to get completely drunk and some people when drunk become extremely destructive – the kitchen door at Kinloch bore a gash from being attacked with a carpet sweeper by one of our visitors whose target had been an agile member of staff, lucky enough to get the door shut between him and his would-be assailant.

There was a door from the public bar into the entrance hall and another, beside the bar, leading towards the kitchen and the combined draughts made this room one of the coldest in Scotland, despite the brightly burning fire. Licensing laws required us to keep the bar open throughout the year and it was this, plus the nuisance factor of the occasional drunken rampage impinging on the peace of the resident guests, which made us decide to close it down, have a restricted licence and turn the room into another sitting room. We closed off the door leading towards the kitchen, immediately cutting down on the cold, and built lots of white-painted bookshelves, transforming it into a very attractive room, invaluable in providing more sitting space for our increasing number of guests.

Guests during Our First Decade

Welcoming the paying public into what is, essentially, your home is strange at first. Godfrey and I have always felt intensely personal about Kinloch and, at the end of our first decade, we made it our home, building a small extension at one end and selling Ostaig House, where we had lived for eight years. From the start, we wanted our guests to feel really welcome – to relax and recharge their batteries, which is surely what a holiday is for. We soon realised that some people staying away from home feel insecure, which is why, I am convinced, regular guests often prefer to stay in the same bedroom each time they visit us.

Among our first guests were a Church of England vicar and his wife, staying in one of our best rooms, and they asked us to send off a couple of postcards they had written to friends. I have to confess that we read them as soon as they were out of sight and were delighted to see how much they enjoyed staying at Kinloch. What they particularly enjoyed was having their shoes cleaned by 'The Lord'. We didn't know which Lord they were referring to but suspected it was Godfrey.

Early on, a remarkable couple came to stay and they would return to Kinloch for two weeks at a time, twice a year, from then onwards. We grew to love them second to my own parents. Roland Shaw, a Bostonian, and his German wife Fee, pronounced 'Fay', abbreviated from Felicitas, were both very tall. At six feet, Fee was always elegant and smelled delicious. Roland was much taller and took shoe size 17. This intrigued our children as they grew older and were allowed into the Shaws' bedroom – always Room 1 – where they could put both feet into one of his shoes. He was a great man not only in stature but in all that he did and had done during his life. He had interrupted his time at Princeton to come to Britain to fight as a bomber pilot during the last World War. After the war, he finished his studies at Princeton, continued at the LSE, joined the American diplomatic service and was posted to Germany, where he met Fee. He became a financial journalist and finally joined the oil industry.

By the time we met the Shaws, Roland had started up his own oil company, Premier Oil, of which he was the chairman and chief executive. They had two daughters, Alexandra and Victoria, and we grew to look forward to their visits keenly. Roland was a workaholic, unable to leave his office behind wherever he went. Fee improvised a desk for him, bringing a cloth with her which she put over a small chest in their bedroom window. In our early years there were no telephones in the guests' bedrooms and the only one was tucked into a cupboard under the main staircase. Folding himself into this cupboard for hours on end must have been dreadfully uncomfortable but dear Roland always joked about it. Along with a number of our other regular guests, he heaved a sigh of relief when, after about twelve years, we installed telephones in each bedroom.

Another two favourite guests who arrived in our first or second year were schoolteachers from the prestigious King Edward's School in Birmingham. One taught botany, the other classics. Roz and Jean came to stay every following summer until last year when, for the first time, they decided to remain at home. During their visits, they would spend a day with us and then, heroically, plan a day to take our three girls off on a trip of fun combined with education. Our son Hugo, who was born in 1982, longed to be allowed to join them but was deemed too young until he was about seven, when he was permitted to go too. Roz and Jean returned slightly bewildered by how much he knew about wild mushrooms, courtesy of Godfrey, and by how keen he was to learn anything he was taught unlike, it must be said, our girls.

We knew and loved so many of our guests and I've always

maintained that pretty well 99 per cent of people are very nice but the remaining 1 per cent can be stinkers. There were always surprises throughout our forty years, perhaps more so at the beginning when, in our naivety, we never expected the unexpected. For instance, we took a reservation for a single man who duly arrived in an Aston Martin over which everyone drooled but, disappointingly, he didn't live up to the glamour of his car. He arrived in the front hall, took his suitcase from whoever was carrying it and proceeded to unpack armfuls of his clothing right there in the hall. Our polite suggestion that this would be better done in his bedroom fell on deaf ears. Other guests arriving and having to step around him and the increasing piles of clothing on the floor looked amazed in case it was house rules for everyone to unpack in the front hall. Eventually we got him and his belongings to his allotted bedroom and he seemed fairly normal from then on until his departure, when he decided to go by bus and asked us to look after his Aston Martin. To choose to travel by one of the infrequent buses rather than his superb car seemed eccentric, to say the least, but off he went and we wondered when we would ever see him again. It was quite a responsibility being put in charge of an Aston Martin and, as far as I remember, he didn't even leave us the keys. Eventually he must have posted these to us because he requested that someone drive it to somewhere in England, which we arranged. He was completely harmless but distinctly odd.

Family Life

Going back to the beginning of our lives as hoteliers, in October 1975 our daughter Isabella was born in Edinburgh, where Alexandra had been born a couple of years before. My parents came to stay with us in the flat we rented for the few weeks before and just after her birth, and my mother and I drove home with Isabella in the carrycot on the back seat. This was after our move into Ostaig, where Godfrey was born and brought up, before we made Kinloch our home, my mother-in-law having transformed Gardener's Cottage into a very nice house which she renamed Armadale House.

We had two dogs, another Cavalier King Charles spaniel, Blenheim in colour, called Audrey but known as Piglet. Godfrey has a way with names – every two- and four-legged member of our family has several, none of which bears the least resemblance to their given name but each, presumably, having an origin. Isabella is and always has been known as Bop, which goes back to when she first started to talk and referred to her 'boppom'. Meriel, our third daughter, who was born in Skye in 1978, is still known as 'Mactoot' and that is the name which pops on to the screen of my mobile phone whenever she rings. Hugo, who was born in 1982, is known by any variation on Luigi. Goodness knows how that began but, when in teasing mood, his sisters have been known to convert this to 'sewage', to rhyme with Luig, pronounced 'Lewage'. To this day, Alexandra, who was known as 'Wit' for ages, never calls Godfrey and me Daddy and Mummy but always Svar and Fume, and again I have no idea why. Meriel calls me 'Marmaduke' when she is being polite and 'MF' – which I shan't translate – when she isn't. My mother-in-law was always known as 'Moo' and, very soon after our marriage, Godfrey renamed my parents 'Mamby and Pape' – close friends still refer to them as such. He also calls my darling old pa 'Monsieur', which had something to do with a black beret, many, many years ago.

We had a succession of mother's helps, some wonderful, some not, and looking after the children was a constant source of worry when we lived at Ostaig. It was a lovely house, with the beach at the bottom of the small hill in front, but this worried me too, especially after the day when Alexandra went missing with her friend Verity, who was staying, both aged five or six. They were eventually spotted having a lovely time on the rocks, with the waves crashing around the base in the raging storm.

When Alexandra was small, there was no playschool and we

didn't have television. It was no wonder, then, that she had three imaginary friends who were very real to her and there were times when Godfrey and I thought they were real too. The main one was called Jo-anne, who was always on the roof or teetering on the brink of somewhere dangerous – real adrenalin-surging stuff was our life with Jo-anne. These imaginary friends faded with the start of primary school, which Alexandra took to like a duck to water.

With our many close friends whose families, like our own, were ever growing in number, there were several unforgettable incidents, including the time when Sue Loudon, now Coombes, and her sons, Gavin and Jamie, were staying with us. Gavin, my godson and profoundly deaf, was Alexandra's age and Jamie was Meriel's. All five children – Alexandra, Isabella, Meriel, Gavin and Jamie – played together well despite the difference in their ages. On this visit, Gavin had just been fitted with hearing aids which had no spare parts. Imagine how I felt when they came in for tea and both Gavin's hearing aids were missing. It turned out that our girls had buried them in the sandpit. The miracle is that we all remained such good friends.

It was always fun when our old friends John and Mary FitzGerald came to stay with their four children, who were similar in age to ours, their eldest, Johnny, being Godfrey's godson. John and Mary helped out on several occasions when we were short staffed at Kinloch, as did many other friends, who often proved more adept at whatever they kindly turned their hands to than we ever were.

In common with most working mothers, I lived with a constant feeling of guilt and, to this day, I feel I could have been a better mother. The difficulty of being torn between work and children eased to some extent when we sold Ostaig and moved into Kinloch in 1982. The extension we built included a large living room/kitchen with glass doors opening in to the garden, three bedrooms, a bathroom and an extra loo with a basin upstairs. Leaving Ostaig was a huge slog and involved clearing out three generations of Macdonalds but somehow we did it and left the old house spotless with a big jug of daffodils in the kitchen for the family who had bought it. They've gone now and Duncan MacInnes from Skye and his wife Polly are there. It is good to think of them and their family enjoying the old house.

Much to everyone's surprise, including our own, our move to Kinloch brought no regrets. Twice during the subsequent years I have dreamed we were back in Ostaig and I've woken up both times feeling a massive weight of depression and then huge relief once I realised that it had only been a dream. Why? I think because our years at Ostaig, during which we had many happy times, were also years fraught with angst. There was the financial nightmare following Godfrey's father's death and, on top of that, the Clan fund-raising, which had been an endless, thankless source of problems, disrupting family life and draining our energy. Plus, Godfrey and I were continually shuttling between Ostaig and Kinloch so, by the time we sat down, exhausted, to supper it was usually nearly 11 p.m. Our move to Kinloch therefore came as a huge relief.

We lived over the shop, as it were, which seemed much easier but, inevitably, at a price – a total loss of privacy. None of the staff seemed to understand that we weren't available twenty-four hours a day or that we should be afforded a measure of privacy. We soon readjusted to this very public life, however, and never quite realised what an intrusion every knock on our door was, for whatever trivial reason, until after we had moved on.

The West Highland Free Press

The birth of a newspaper is always exciting but, if it happens to be born locally, as was the *West Highland Free Press* to us, it can prove to be a nightmare and this one certainly did for us. There is a certain element of 'left-wingery' which loves to stereotype and, being who we were, we were easy targets for both ridicule and mockery. It was hard but we felt we had no choice but to ignore the weekly jibes the paper was hurling at us just because of Godfrey's birth. Local friends urged us to sue them or retaliate by writing letters, but we firmly believed that ignoring them was the best line of action and, in those days, it wouldn't have made a blind bit of difference to how they felt about us, nor would it have prevented them from springing into print about us for the least, or even no, reason. One front-page headline stands out in my memory: 'Godfrey, so-called Lord Macdonald . . .' He wasn't 'so-called' – he *was* Lord Macdonald! They ignored the fact that we were contributing to the economy in Skye in no small way, as well as employing local people when jobs weren't easy to find. We grew to dread Thursdays – publication day – and were always thankful that Godfrey's father never lived to see the *West Highland Free Press* days, as they would have lampooned him into the grave.

The paper took up criticising the formation of the Clan Donald Lands Trust with gusto. They cast Godfrey in the role of the wicked Clan Chief who was just getting members of the Clan to fork out money to pay off his vast debt, resulting from two lots of death duties – 'Clan Chief Denies Lining his Sporran' is just one typical headline that springs to mind. They couldn't see that the formation of the CDLT was going to play a major role locally by providing a centre for Clan Donald which would provide employment for residents in the neighbourhood. Nor could they realise that, had the estate been sold on the open market, it would realise very much more than we could ever hope to get from the sale to the Clan. The *West Highland Free Press* were completely blinkered in their image of Godfrey and what he stood for – from a historical point of view, he represented everything they abhorred. Their relentless battering of Godfrey in their weekly paper was so persistent that it drew national attention. Godfrey was contacted by the then producer of the BBC1 evening news programme to see if he would be willing to be interviewed, at Kinloch, and take part in a debate with the paper's founding editor, Brian Wilson. Godfrey agreed and the meeting and interview took place in the bar, the room to the right of the front door when you enter Kinloch. It was a highly charged atmosphere, to put it mildly, and so was their discussion, but what surprised them both was that, face to face, they actually got on quite well. They are the same age – Godfrey born and brought up on Skye and loyal to the island to his core, Brian born and brought up also on the west coast but in Argyll. The outcome was that Brian Wilson and Godfrey respected each other's opinions and the real venom had been drawn. Thereafter, relations with the *West Highland Free Press* never again plumbed the depths of gratuitous insult that existed so regularly before their televised meeting.

Brian Wilson still writes an important column each week but, since those early days, he has also been a Labour MP for many years. Time moves on and extreme feelings mellow with age and that is how our relationship with the *West Highland Free Press* seems to have settled these days, thank goodness. In fact, when Kinloch was awarded its Michelin Star thirty-six years later, their editor wrote about it and about Godfrey and me and our work in such a way that, when I rang up to thank him, I was in tears (see plate section). That article meant more to us than anything written in any publication, before or since. It was such a genuine tribute and I could cry now, just remembering it.

There was one *Free Press* journalist with whom we struck up friendship – Roger Hutchinson. He wrote the sports page and still reviews books for them. In those days, he lived in Breakish with his beautiful partner, Caroline, a typesetter with the *Free Press*. They often came to Kinloch for bar lunches and we always enjoyed their visits. We don't see them so much since they moved to the island of Raasay but, in those far-off days, they were the only good thing, as far as we were concerned, about the *West Highland Free Press*.

Recipes
from Our First Decade

Kinloch Mousse

Serves 6

---

600 ml (1 pint) jellied chicken consommé – I am not even sure that this is available
   now, so I would substitute 600 ml (1 pint) good chicken stock and 4 leaves of
   gelatine soaked in cold water for 10 minutes
450 g (1 lb) Philadelphia cream cheese – these days I would use the low-fat type
1 rounded tsp medium-strength curry powder
1 fat garlic clove, skinned and chopped finely
small handful of parsley, stalks discarded
18 large prawns, cooked and shelled – these are part garnish and at the same
   time an integral part of this first course

Heat the stock and lift the soaked gelatine leaves from their
water bath, leaving behind all the water, and drop them into the
hot stock. Swirl the pan until the gelatine dissolves, then leave
the liquid in a cool place until the stock starts to gel, when it is
cold.

Put the cream cheese, curry powder and chopped garlic
into a food processor with the gelling stock and whiz till
smooth. Add the parsley to the contents of the processor and
whiz briefly to break up the parsley but not to pulverise it
completely.

Divide this mixture evenly between 6 ramekins and put 3
large prawns on top of each. Loosely cover the 6 ramekins with
cling film and put in the fridge till 20 minutes before serving.

I like to serve Melba toast with this.

Godfrey salivates at the mention of this, even now, all these
years later, and it was a staple on our menu, which we changed
daily. We tried never to duplicate anything during the length of
stay of any of our guests but, on many occasions, we were asked
to repeat certain dishes.

Eggs Niçoise

Serves 6

—

6 large eggs, hardboiled, shelled and chopped – I do this using a sharp knife in a
    large bowl

300 ml (½ pint) vegetable or chicken stock – or use a good substitute such as
    Marigold powder made up with boiling water

4 leaves of gelatine soaked in cold water for 10 minutes, then drained of their cold
    water bath and dissolved in the hot stock

150 ml (¼ pint) double cream whipped but not stiffly – today, I use crème fraîche
    instead

150 ml (¼ pint) home-made mayonnaise

1 tsp anchovy essence

1 tbsp Worcester sauce

—

For garnishing:

—

1 tin anchovy fillets, drained and each cut in half lengthways

10 stoned top-quality black olives – I like Kalamata olives best – each cut in slivers

—

Add the cold, gelling stock to the chopped hardboiled eggs in
the mixing bowl. Then mix in the whipped cream – or crème
fraîche – mayonnaise, anchovy essence and Worcester sauce.
Taste and add a small amount of salt if you think it is needed – I
don't think it will be, as the anchovy essence and Worcester
sauce contribute sufficient saltiness. Season with black pepper
and spoon and scrape into a serving bowl. You can, if you
prefer, put the mixture into individual small bowls or dishes –
we used ramekins all those years ago. Leave to set.

Then lay the slivers of anchovy fillet in lines across, then
diagonally, to give diamond shapes. Put a piece of black olive in
each of the diamond shapes.

I make this recipe to this day and it is good served with a
tomato salad.

Deep-fried Cheese Beignets with Tomato Sauce

Serves 6

For the tomato sauce:

———

2 tbsp olive oil

1 onion, skinned and chopped

1 stick of celery, peeled with a potato peeler to get rid of the stringy bits, then chopped

2 x 400 g tins of chopped tomatoes

1 level tsp sugar

1 tsp salt

15 or so grinds black pepper

———

Heat the olive oil and fry the chopped onion and celery together, stirring occasionally, for 3–5 minutes over moderate heat. Then add the contents of the tins of chopped tomatoes, the sugar, salt and black pepper. Simmer very gently for 7–10 minutes, then take the pan off the heat and cool slightly before whizzing the contents to a smooth texture. The sauce should be served warm beneath the cheese beignets.

For the beignets:

———

50 g (2 oz) butter

2 rounded tbsp plain flour

450 ml (¾ pint) milk

1 rounded tsp English mustard

dash of Worcester sauce

175 g (6 oz) grated cheese – I use Mull cheddar

½ tsp salt

15 or so grinds black pepper

1 grating nutmeg

2 large egg yolks

sunflower oil for deep-frying

———

Don't be afraid of deep-frying – you just need to heat oil to a depth of about 10 cm (4 in) in a deep saucepan. Fry only 4–5 beignets at a time.

Melt the butter in a saucepan and stir in the flour. Let this cook for a minute before gradually adding the milk, stirring all the time. Stir in the mustard and Worcester sauce – you will have a stiff sauce. Let it bubble for a minute then take the pan off the heat and stir in the grated cheese, which will melt in the heat of the sauce, and stir in the salt, pepper and nutmeg. Beat in the egg yolks.

Leave this to cool completely before deep-frying.

Heat the oil till very hot. Drop a bit of bread in to test that it's hot enough. If the bread immediately sizzles, it is. Take it out before frying the beignets.

With two teaspoons, scoop walnut-sized blobs of the cold cheese mixture and drop them into the very hot oil. They will bob around and quickly make a crispy exterior, turn them over during their 2–3 minutes' cooking time then, with a slotted spoon, scoop them out of the oil on to a warm dish lined with 2–3 thicknesses of absorbent kitchen paper and continue deep-frying the blobs of cheese mixture to transform them into beignets.

When all the mixture is used up, reheat the smooth sauce (to which you can, if you like, add ½ tsp dried chilli flakes) and put a spoonful on to each of 6 warmed plates. Put 3 beignets on the sauce and serve.

Spiced Lamb with Apricots

Serves 6

3 tbsp olive oil

1.2 kg (2½ lbs) lamb, trimmed of fat and cut into even-sized bits about 2 cm (1 in) in size

4 onions, skinned, halved and very finely sliced

1 fat clove of garlic, skinned and diced

1 just rounded tbsp flour

1 tsp salt

20 or so grinds black pepper

2 tsp coriander seeds

2 tsp cumin seeds

1 tsp powdered cinnamon

220 g (8 oz) no-soak dried apricots, each cut in half

600 ml (1 pint) stock

In an ovenproof pan with a lid, heat the olive oil and brown the pieces of lamb all over, a small amount at a time, scooping them as they brown into a warm dish. Then, when all the lamb is browned, add the finely sliced onions to the remaining oil in the pan and cook them, stirring occasionally, for 5–7 minutes. Add the garlic during this time.

Put the spices and the salt and pepper together in a pestle and mortar and pound them – if you don't have a pestle and mortar, put them into a deep small bowl and bash them with the end of a rolling pin. Add them to the onions and garlic in the pan and fry for a couple of minutes, then stir in the flour. Stir it well into the onions, then gradually add the stock, stirring all the time until it reaches simmering point. Return the browned lamb to the pan along with the apricots and, when the liquid reaches simmering point once more, cover the pan with its lid and cook in a moderate oven at 350°F, 180°C or gas mark 4 for 1 hour. Then take the pan out of the oven, cool and store in the fridge for up to 2 days. Before serving, take the pan from the fridge and allow the contents to come up to room temperature for half an hour. Reheat on top of the cooker to simmering point before cooking the spiced lamb stew at the same moderate oven temperature as for its initial cooking for a further half an hour.

This is one of the recipes I made during my first-ever Highland Show demonstrations and I like it served with boiled basmati rice and a green vegetable, such as Savoy cabbage or steamed Brussels sprouts.

Coronation Chicken (my version)

Serves 6

---

1 chicken weighing upwards of 1.5 kg (3½ lbs)
1 onion
1 stick celery
1 carrot

Hackneyed though this dish must seem, it is loved by so many, me included, and this recipe is, I think, the best.

Simmer the chicken in water with the onion, celery and carrots for about 1 hour until the meat pulls away from the leg bones. Then allow the chicken to cool in the liquid. Strip the cold chicken from the carcase. Throw away the skin but put the bones back into the liquid the chicken was cooked in and simmer for a couple of hours to produce a really good chicken stock.

For the coronation sauce:

---

300 ml (½ pint) double cream, whipped but not stiffly
300 ml (½ pint) mayonnaise – home-made is best
1 tbsp white wine vinegar
2 fairly level tsp medium-strength curry powder
1 tbsp runny honey
1 tsp salt
15 or so grinds black pepper

Fold the whipped cream and mayonnaise together.

Mix the white wine vinegar, curry powder and runny honey together. Then mix this into the cream and mayonnaise, with the salt and black pepper.

Mix this sauce thoroughly into the pieces of cooked chicken – the aim is to coat each bit of chicken with sauce.

Heap the coated chicken onto a serving plate or ashet and surround with assorted salad leaves.

This is particularly good with the following rice salad.

Rice, Almond and Grape Salad

Serves 6

———

75 g (3 oz) flaked almonds
350 g (12 oz) basmati rice
175 g (6 oz) seedless red or black grapes, halved
4 tbsp extra virgin olive oil
rind of 1 lemon, finely grated
juice of ½ lemon
1 tsp salt
15 or so grinds black pepper
1 tbsp parsley and chives, finely chopped and mixed together

———

Dry-fry the flaked almonds till lightly toasted, then allow them to cool.

Simmer the rice in salted water till tender – about 7 minutes. Pour off the cooking liquid, run cold water through the rice and then drain in a large fine-meshed sieve. Tip the drained rice into a mixing bowl and add all the other ingredients, including the toasted flaked almonds.

Mix everything together thoroughly and pile onto an ashet or serving dish.

Pork Fillet with Apples, Leeks and Cider

Serves 6

———

2 pork fillets with a combined weight of approx. 1.15 kg (2½ lb)
3 tbsp olive oil
6 medium-sized leeks
4 good eating apples, such as Cox's
1 rounded tbsp flour
600 ml (1 pint) dry cider or unsweetened apple juice
1 tsp salt
20 or so grinds black pepper
1 grating nutmeg

———

Trim the pork fillet and cut it into slices about 1 cm (just under
½ in) thick, to give 15–16 slices.

Remove any tatty outer leaves from the leeks and trim
them at both ends. Slice each leek on the diagonal into 1 cm
thicknesses. Peel, core and quarter the apples. Cut each apple
quarter into 3 slices.

In a wide sauté or casserole pan heat 2 tablespoons of the
olive oil and fry the sliced leeks over moderate heat for 7–8
minutes, stirring occasionally. Then add the sliced apples, dust
in the flour and cook for a couple of minutes before gradually
stirring in the cider or apple juice. When the sauce bubbles, add
the salt, pepper and nutmeg.

In a frying pan or sauté pan, heat the remaining olive oil
and, over high heat, fry each slice of pork fillet on either side
for a couple of minutes, removing them to the leek and apple
sauce as they are browned.

Cook the pork fillets in the leek and apple mixture in the
covered casserole or sauté pan at a moderate oven temperature
– 350°F, 180°C or gas mark 4 – for 40 minutes.

This is particularly good accompanied by well-mashed
potatoes, beaten with a tablespoon of horseradish, and a green
vegetable such as Savoy cabbage or kale.

Orange Caramel Trifle

Serves 6

For the sponge cake:

———

2 large eggs
50 g (2 oz) caster sugar
50 g (2 oz) self-raising flour, sieved twice

———

Whisk up the eggs and caster sugar till so thick that, when you drizzle it over the surface, it leaves a trail.

Sieve the twice-sieved flour for a third time into the egg and sugar mixture and, using a flat whisk, fold it thoroughly into the mousse-like mixture.

Line the base of a non-stick square cake tin with baking parchment. Pour and scrape the sponge cake mixture into this and bake at a moderate heat – 350°F, 180°C or gas mark 4 – for 20–25 minutes.

Take it out of the oven – it should have shrunk from the sides of the cake tin very slightly – tip onto a cooling rack and leave till cold.

This was one of our yummiest puds in our early days. I made the sponge cake from scratch but you could buy a well-made sponge cake from a reputable baker.

For the custard:

———

300 ml (1 pint) single cream
4 large egg yolks
75 g (3 oz) caster sugar
1 tsp vanilla extract

———

Heat the cream in a heavy-based saucepan over a moderate heat.

Beat together the yolks and sugar till very pale and thick,

then mix some of the hot cream into this. Scrape the mixture into the saucepan with the rest of the hot cream. Over moderate heat and stirring all the time, cook the custard until it thickens. Beware of overheating it as this could cause the custard to curdle. You just need to make sure you use a heavy-based pan and keep stirring all the time. Add the vanilla extract and take the pan off the heat when the custard is thickened.

For the caramel:

———

75 g (3 oz) granulated sugar

———

Put the sugar into a saucepan over moderate heat and shake the pan from time to time, but do not stir, ever. Gradually, the sugar will start to dissolve and, when it becomes molten and amber in colour, pour it onto a baking tray. Leave till cold.

When cold, put the baking tray into a deep, empty sink. Cover the caramel with a sheet of baking parchment and bash it with a rolling pin till you have small shards of caramel – by doing it in the sink and by covering the caramel surface with parchment, you avoid getting bits of caramel flying around your kitchen.

Store the bits of caramel in a screw-top glass jar.

———

4 good oranges – navel when in season

———

Take the skin and pith off the oranges using a sharp serrated knife. Cut the oranges into segments, slicing in towards the centre of each orange and separating the orange flesh from the membranes, which can sometimes be quite tough.

———

300 ml (½ pint) double cream, whipped but not at all stiffly

———

To assemble the trifle, put a layer of sponge cake in the base of a wide glass or china dish. Cover with the orange segments. Spoon the cold vanilla custard sauce over the sponge and orange segments, then spoon the sloppy whipped cream over the entire surface and scatter tiny shards of caramel over the cream. It's best to do this several hours in advance. Cover the dish with cling film and store it in a cool place till required. A larder would be ideal but, if it must be the fridge, be sure to take the trifle out and bring it up to room temperature at least 30 minutes before serving. Delicious!

Dark Chocolate Brandy Cake

Serves 8

---

75 g (3 oz) sultanas – the largest plump ones
3 tbsp brandy
220 g (8 oz) butter
220 g (8 oz) dark chocolate
2 large eggs
75 g (3 oz) caster sugar
75 g (3 oz) walnuts, chopped
220 g (8 oz) crushed digestive biscuits
8 walnut halves to garnish

Put the sultanas in the brandy in a bowl, cover with cling film and leave to soak for several hours.

Melt the butter and dark chocolate together.

Beat together the eggs and caster sugar, beating until the mixture is very pale and very thick.

Line a 900 g (2 lb) loaf tin with baking parchment so that the base and short sides of the tin are covered.

Fold the thick chocolate and butter mixture together with the thick mousse-like egg and sugar combination and fold the chopped walnuts, the brandy and sultanas and the crushed digestives into this. Mix thoroughly, then pour into the lined loaf tin, smooth the surface, cover the tin with cling film and leave it in the fridge for several hours till cold.

To serve, turn out the chocolate brandy cake and peel off the strip of baking parchment.

At evenly spaced intervals push the walnut halves into the surface, in a row down the centre, and serve in thick slices.

This is in a league of its own when it comes to the chocolate and biscuit combination – it's really more of a pudding than any tiffin-type of similar tray bake. It featured regularly on the menu as a pud during our first and second decades and it remains one of Godfrey's favourites – but without the brandy. It can be made up to two days in advance, providing that it is kept in a cold larder or in the fridge.

Ginger Biscuit Log

Serves 8

-----

600 ml (1 pint) double cream
2 tbsp syrup from jar of stem ginger (see below)
150 ml (¼ pint) Crabbie's or Stone's ginger wine
150 ml (¼ pint) cold water
2 packets of gingernut biscuits

For garnishing:

-----

8 pieces of stem ginger, drained of the syrup and sliced into fine slivers
75 g (3 oz) dark chocolate, coarsely grated

This is very much a pudding of the times but with embellishment all my own.

Whip the cream with the 2 tablespoons of ginger syrup till fairly stiff.

Mix the ginger wine and water together and pour onto a plate. Dip each gingernut into this. Then spread them thinly with whipped cream and stack them in two towers.

When all the biscuits have been treated like this, lay the towers flat and side by side and coat entirely with the rest of the whipped cream. Scatter the grated dark chocolate and the slivers of ginger over the log.

Leave for several hours in the fridge before slicing to serve.

Part Two

Our Second Decade
1983–1993

Me, a Food Writer!

As I have already written, our second decade began with selling Ostaig House, adding on to Kinloch and moving, and I've mentioned the relief despite the loss of privacy. Hugo was fourteen months old when we moved, Meriel four, Isabella seven and Alexandra nine. The two oldest were at school at Ferindonald, the primary school for those living in Sleat. As well as living in the extension we'd built on, we were occupying two of the hotel bedrooms. We decided it was time to extend again and we built on a long sitting room with two bedrooms above it.

This decade saw a great deal of change in my life, including my conversion to Catholicism. The League of Friends of the MacKinnon Memorial Hospital in Broadford was founded, with John Kubale as treasurer, Barbara Reyntiens of Seathrift Croft Enterprise, the flower shop in Kyle of Lochalsh, as secretary and me as chairman. It was during this decade that I began my writing career and we started our cooking demonstrations at Kinloch, as well as further afield. Towards the end of it came the death of Godfrey's mother followed by Godfrey's treatment for and recovery from alcoholism, which was a new beginning of life for him and for the rest of the family.

Me, a food writer! One day in 1983, I was doing the flowers in the big drawing room when one of our guests started chatting to me. He was Eric Baird, the then editor of *Scottish Field*, and, to my utter astonishment, he invited me to become their food writer. My immediate response was that I couldn't possibly – I had never done anything like that before – but he insisted that I could do it. He certainly took a gamble, brave man, and, terrified and thrilled, I agreed to have a go. I've always loved writing letters, and I hate the way that impersonal emails, useful and immediate as they are, seem to have taken over from written correspondence. Letters can be kept and treasured and reread. What will become the vital material for biographies and autobiographies with no letters to refer to and include in a book?

I wrote my first article for the *Scottish Field* while in America for a Clan Donald USA Annual General Meeting. I began worrying about every word until, gradually, I relaxed a bit and the writing became a pleasure. Then, some time afterwards, to my complete surprise, the eminent food writer, broadcaster and founder of BBC Radio 4's *The Food Programme*, Derek Cooper, rang me up to say I had been awarded the Glenfiddich Cookery Writer of the Year Award for my *Scottish Field* column. I was astonished. With no idea of what to expect, I went to London for the award lunch, so nervous I almost didn't dare go in by myself. They gave me a handsome gold medal. I was thrilled, never having won anything before in my life apart from once backing a winner in the Grand National. All I remember of the lunch was a huge pyramid of cherry tomatoes with a creamy dressing trickling down them – effective to look at but I don't think I actually ate anything.

With this award came an offer of a contract to write two books from the then new Century Publishing House, now part of Random House. The present chairman of Random House is Gail Rebuck, who was the editor of my first book, *Seasonal Cooking from the Isle of Skye*. I was terrified of her, but she was an excellent editor and taught me much that has stood me in good stead ever since. Poor Gail, her Achilles heel was discovered when she came to Skye, early one May, with a photographer to get a picture for the cover of the book. I had broken my ankle quite badly the week before but hadn't told her because I didn't want to upset the arrangements. The weather was bad, the only gap in the rain being very early one morning. I leapt – well, slight exaggeration with my leg in plaster – out of bed, put a bin liner on my plaster to keep it dry and gathered food for the photograph. We made our way down to the shore, where the photographer was all set up with his camera, lights, etc. He got a photograph just before the rain started once more and we hobbled back up to the house for breakfast. But poor Gail, being in such a remote place disturbed her so much that she took to her bed for the rest of the day.

The publicist for Century, Susan Lamb, was fun – very much a livewire – and she became a good friend. She even named her racehorse after Kinloch. The book was beautifully produced and sold well. Then I had to get straight on with the next one, *Sweet Things*, containing recipes for puddings, cakes, biscuits, jams and jellies galore. Sadly, Century rather lost interest with this one because they were also publishing a book by a woman who lived such a healthy existence somewhere in Cornwall that she even delivered her own babies, effortlessly, at home, all due to the fact that she only ate raw food and sugar never entered her diet – certainly not her recipes. Poor *Sweet Things* was therefore rather ignored to begin with, but most people do love an indulgence and the book is still available, which shows that, for many people, a raw-food existence with no chocolate isn't an option.

I'm ashamed to say that I now became too big for my boots. Roddy Martine was then the editor of *Scottish Field*. He had always been a good friend – in fact, he had been at our wedding in 1969 – and I started badgering him to raise my salary, which he couldn't do, so, eventually and deservedly, I was replaced by another food writer and it served me right. About this time, I was offered a column with the esteemed *Press and Journal*, Scotland's oldest daily newspaper and, until early 2012, still published in broadsheet format, and I have written for the '*P&J*' ever since.

I was offered a contract to write a book called *Delicious Fish* for Grafton and the same year I was approached by Harrods to write their *Book of Entertaining*. When it came to doing the photographs for this, two huge vans arrived at Kinloch, bearing a vast amount of beautiful props from Harrods. There were plates, glasses, cutlery and all the decorations for a Christmas tree – in fact, everything one could possibly want to cover all the recipes within the book. The photographer had her assistant, a stylist, with her and a home economist called Maxine Clark, who became a great friend. Maxine is a brilliant cook, as well as being tremendous fun. We spent such a week, working so hard, and at the end of it all we had some wonderful photographs. I think that book, though long out of print, was simply beautiful. To my secret sorrow at the time, the stylist carefully and meticulously counted every single item from Harrods back into the van – I was rather hoping a few of the items might get forgotten.

Next came an offer from Ebury Press to write *The Chocolate Book*. This was right up my street – my addiction to chocolate had definitely been inherited from both my parents, who loved chocolate too. It was written in conjunction with Terry's of York, famous for their dark chocolate. Some years later, when we took the contents of the shop we started at Kinloch some time later to the Mary Howard Christmas Fair on York racecourse, I found the Terry's chocolate factory was behind us and savoured the wonderful chocolaty aroma filling the air. Then came the sad year when there was no chocolate fragrance – Terry's had closed down and the factory was silent. Another tragic event happened in November 2008 when Mary Howard was killed in a road accident near Hullavington Airfield, one of the sites of that year's fairs. A tireless charity fundraiser, Mary started the Mary Howard Christmas Fairs in the late 1980s and the Howard family have continued to hold the annual fairs in the run-up to Christmas each year. Hugely popular, the fairs are always held on race-courses, such as York and Sandown, as well as at the disused airfield at Hullavington. The fairs have raised over £1 million for various charities, notably the NSPCC.

The first edition of *The Chocolate Book* was beautifully presented with a white cover and gold writing, reflecting the sumptuous recipes within. It was then reprinted with a hideous, garish cover in blue, milk-chocolate brown and pink. Sadly, many people don't realise that the author often has little say in the end result of a book and this was the case with *The Chocolate Book*.

During this time, I also wrote *More Seasonal Cooking*, a sequel to *Seasonal Cooking*. I have always cooked with the season and deplore imported out-of-season foods. For instance, asparagus imported from South America is absolutely wrong in flavour, texture and every other way, compared with our asparagus in season. Strawberries can now also be bought all year round, as they are imported when not in season here. The incomers look the part but taste of acidic water, misleading people into thinking that this is how all strawberries taste. We ought to be patient and wait for British asparagus and locally grown strawberries. Supermarkets have much to answer for and a disregard of the seasons is one of them. Steam comes from my ears when I search for British-grown apples and pears in the autumn and can only find so many imported varieties. Seasonality in everything we eat has always been of paramount importance to me.

I then wrote *Suppers*, which proved extremely popular, followed by *Lunches*, after which I was asked to write a book on Scottish food. *Claire Macdonald's Scotland: The Best of Scottish Food and Drink* included recipes and also, most importantly, details about the food producers. It turned out to be a beautiful book and, had it been properly published in the United States, it could have sold like the proverbial hotcakes. For some reason – and I never did find out what it was – the copies that were destined for the US market never made it to the bookshop shelves. A very busy schedule doing cooking dems and some TV work in New York and New Jersey had been organised, and it was maddening to have to tell would-be buyers that the book wasn't available. However, it certainly sold very well in this country and many of our guests at Kinloch from all over the world bought copies to take home with them.

Then Minty Dallmeyer and I compiled a large book, *The Claire Macdonald Cookbook*, which has proved to be immensely popular and was followed in turn by *Simply Seasonal*, *Entertaining Solo* and finally *Fish*. When I wrote *Fish*, twenty-two years had passed since my first fish book for Grafton, *Delicious Fish*, and I had learned a vast amount about fish and the cooking of it during those years, many of the results of which are in *Fish*. During these years, I had discovered how versatile fish and shellfish are and how adventurous one can be in combining other foods and flavours with them which, all those years ago, I would never have thought of using. To give a couple of examples, using red wine and prunes in a sauce for monkfish, or lime and coriander and soya sauce with cod – both of which seem unremarkable as I write, but forty years ago, when salmon, for instance, was served either hot with hollandaise sauce or cold with mayonnaise, such adventurous food combinations would have been unthinkable. Life in the kitchen can be very exciting!

During the early 1980s, I was asked to write a book for the Asda supermarket chain on vegetable recipes and this was another example of the times. My recipes were kept on a tight rein because freshly ground black pepper and fresh garlic were deemed elitist – not what most people used. The week-long photographic session in a studio in Harrow consisted of extremely dated methods to get the food to look good in the pictures, with the result being that, at the end of each morning, surrounded by cooked vegetable dishes, we couldn't eat any of them and had to send out for sandwiches for lunch. This had nothing to do with disliking the actual dishes or the quality of the ingredients but because the food had been brushed with things like washing-up liquid mixed with Marmite, rendering it inedible but giving a good grilled appearance for the camera. Food photography has changed dramatically during the decades that I have been writing – as has the accessibility of foods, wherever you live.

I was asked to compile a book featuring some of the best Scottish hotels and restaurants in the Highlands and Islands. The idea was that each chef would supply three recipes – a starter, main and pudding – and I would write about what I found so attractive about how each establishment was run, as well as talking a little about their geographical settings. However, I always felt that *Scottish Highland Hospitality*, as this book was named, was stilted because I wasn't allowed enough space to say what I wanted. I selected several hotels and restaurants that I thought might be suitable for inclusion in the book and visited all my chosen places personally to assess them. On one island trip to visit two of them, Godfrey and Hugo accompanied me, but one, in the most beautiful spot, high above a white beach, was not at all what we had expected. For a start, we were three of only five guests. Our rooms were damp, our beds damper still and, when we went down for dinner, our host was effusive to the point of being hectic. I asked to see the wine list and he pointed to five bottles, a mixture of red and white, on the windowsill and said, 'There they are!' We had a bottle of tepid white wine with our never-to-be-forgotten dinner, about which our host was completely honest. 'Rat!' he proclaimed, explaining that, when he had a collection of old vegetables, of any type, he chucked them into the pot together and called them 'rat', his version of ratatouille!

Obviously, his establishment couldn't be included in my book, although it would have been fun to do so. It was publicised on the tourist market, however, and my blood ran cold imagining guests arriving there and thinking that it represented Scottish hospitality. Luckily, the places I did include in the book were and, in most cases, still are prime examples of the excellence to be found throughout Scotland in the hotel, restaurant and bed-and-breakfast business.

I have been incredibly lucky in that I have been able to combine my cookbook-writing career with that of a journalistic food writer. I hold my breath as I write this, but I have never been out of regular work as a food writer. Most probably, having written that, the phone will ring to tell me that the editor has decided that one of the two newspapers for which I write has decided to dispense with my services but, when that inevitable day comes, my main concern will be that I shall miss my readers. I rarely go out without someone coming up to me and discussing food or a particular recipe, and I get letters and emails from people either asking for help with an occasion or with a recipe. I find it a great privilege to have this connection with people who I would otherwise never meet. I have now written for the *Press and Journal* for about thirty-one years and for the *Scotsman* magazine each Saturday for about ten years. Before then, I wrote for the Glasgow *Evening News* and then for the *Herald*. And, for seventeen years, I was the food writer for *The Field*. I still get comments from people I meet through doing cooking demonstrations about my cookery articles in the *Field*, which is gratifying because being dismissed – or sacked, call it what you will, but anyway got rid of – was a severe wound to the pride.

Cooking Demonstrations

Early in the 1980s, we had a journalist, Shirley Flack, staying with her husband Michael Dineen because Shirley was writing a piece about Kinloch for *The Times*. They were extremely nice and we had them for a drink one evening during which we were discussing how we could extend the season which, back then, only ran to five or six months. Shirley asked if I had ever thought of doing cooking demonstrations and holding them at Kinloch, thus enticing guests to Skye during what is known in the tourist trade as the 'shoulder months'. That was the start of many years of cooking dems at Kinloch, all thanks to Shirley Flack. Coincidentally, around this time, I had been invited by our local WRI to give a dem in the hall in the nearby village of Ardvasar and I had also been asked to do the demonstrations at the Royal Highland Show, organised by the *Scotsman* newspaper and run extremely efficiently by the ever-elegant Wendy Jones. And so it was that, with these invitations and Shirley's suggestion, I began my cooking demonstration career.

The Ardvasar dem was probably the most scary of all. Quite why I chose pâtés and terrines as the theme I can't think. But it was the preparation for that, my first-ever demonstration, which set the pattern that I have followed ever since. Not many people realise how much effort lies in the preparation. Somehow I got through the evening, but it was all made worse by the deafening silence during the hour-long ordeal – and it was an ordeal for me. My friend Jo Wattie, the wife of the headmaster at our primary school and herself an extremely good cook, had given a cake-icing dem some months before and had warned me about this and told me how unnerved she had been by the complete silence throughout, broken only, right at the end, as she was finishing writing Merry Christmas in vivid scarlet on a pure white iced cake, when a voice piped up to say, 'You've missed the "r" out of Christmas.' Jo took up a large palette knife and swept all the red writing off the top of the beautiful cake with a flourish, leaving it with a dramatically modernist scarlet, and, white streaked finish.

Although forewarned, I found the silence off-putting and it gave me verbal diarrhoea. As I squelched sausage meat with chopped liver for a terrine, as I stretched streaky bacon rashers to line the tin, as I somehow made pâtés out of mushrooms and sardines and chicken livers – those are only three out of the six recipes I did that evening – I chattered away like mad, feeling the silence ever more oppressive. I think the reason was that, in those days, we weren't used to seeing people cooking except in their kitchens and the audience was somehow cowed. Impossible though it seems now, the days of television cooks were yet to come. Today, you can watch a cooking programme pretty much every day on one of the channels but, back then, it was so rare that perhaps it was a bit awe inspiring.

The Kinloch-based cooking demonstrations were started that autumn. I worked out fourteen recipes, seven for each day and we began the three-night breaks with two days of cooking demonstration which we have run ever since. The format seems successful so we have never changed it, except for dropping two of the recipes and now only doing six per day. The dems are followed by tastings and then lunch after which our guests have the afternoon to themselves to walk, shop, especially down at the wonderful Ragamuffin, on Armadale pier, or snooze by one of the log fires. At the dems, I always have an accomplice, usually Minty. I'm sure it must be surprising to some but our friendship was never dented by working together – in fact, I think it became infinitely stronger. When people work together they often then become friends but being friends and then working together can be tricky – it never was or is with Minty. We have done dems in the strangest places, all over the world, and she knows what I am going to say or what I am thinking before I say it. I would dare to say that we understand one another. Few people seem to comprehend this. Some years ago, someone said to me, 'I hear you are actually allowing Minty to speak during the dems.' This cut me to the quick because I had never intended to give the impression that I allow or don't allow anything and certainly never with Minty. She grinds her teeth in rage when, as invariably happens, people say, 'I want a Minty!' We chat, she and I, during the dems and she prompts me when I forget something. She is mentally a step ahead of me, which can be invaluable.

Sometimes, what I am thinking while am doing a demonstration can be completely divorced from what I am saying. For instance, while I am describing the intricacies of making a roux I might well be thinking, 'That woman with the pretty necklace in the third row looks a bit severe – she must have had a problem with a recipe and she is going to ask me about it afterwards.' The day will surely come when I inadvertently say what I am thinking but it hasn't happened yet, though, with advancing years, I feel sure the day isn't too far distant . . .

The ingredients for the recipes I demonstrate at Kinloch reflect the seasons and, whether at Kinloch or anywhere else, I use these opportunities to speak about food in general and tell people about the unsurpassable quality of Scottish food, which I hold to be the best in the world.

I have another self-appointed role which I use to the full during my dems and that is to encourage people to eat without guilt. We are all so beset by guilt, being endlessly fed news snippets about what is bad for us to eat or drink – virtually everything that gives pleasure, it seems. My message is banish guilt – it is a sin to spoil the enjoyment of, say, a good chocolate éclair while thinking with each mouthful, 'I shouldn't be eating this.' We can eat anything, unless we are allergic, providing we eat in moderation. I glean much of my knowledge of food from listening to programmes such as the early morning *Farming Today*, on Radio 4, a fount of information on all aspects of food as well as farming. I also voraciously read everything I can find regarding food – how it is produced, transported, stored. I absorb and recount everything I have learnt to my guests at cooking dems.

If I found my first demonstration in the Ardvasar Hall frightening, all those year ago, when I accepted Wendy Jones' invitation to do one at the Royal Highland Show, I had no idea how much more terrifying the whole thing would be. Wendy herself could not have been more helpful, in every way. She even reminded me to brush the back of my hair as, apparently, they had had a demonstrator the previous year who had failed to do this and it was seen clearly in the huge mirror. I have the image of an immaculate hairstyle with a bird's nest at the back, completely distracting the guests at each dem. There were four demonstrations each day, with four recipes at each one, and the show ran for four days. I was extremely lucky to be assisted by home economics students from the Queen Margaret College in Edinburgh, who prepared the trays of ingredients for each dem. But students who prepare a tray don't need the adrenalin required beforehand, which is what makes me check and recheck everything for every recipe, so I worked with them, just to make sure. I tend to be fanatical over these details but I've learnt that it is the only way and there can't be any shortcuts. I am ruled by lists.

The Highland Show demonstrations were for about 400 people and I've always suspected that quite a few came just so they could sit down, get the weight off their legs and have a small rest and, certainly, during most dems, one or two dozed off. I found that one session quickly ran into the next and it was vitally important to keep on my toes and be one step ahead. Nothing caused me more panic than not being quite ready when a dem was about to start. I learnt so much during that first year at the

77

Highland Show and will always feel huge gratitude to Wendy Jones for giving me that opportunity. The following year and most years thereafter, she re-invited me. The third week in June meant Royal Highland Show time and I grew to love the buzz of it. It's the largest agricultural show in the United Kingdom and always beautifully organised.

No dem was entirely straightforward. No matter how hard I tried to remember every single item for all of the recipes, I am far from infallible. Beneath each seat was a raffle ticket and, when I'd finished demonstrating the four recipes, four raffle tickets were drawn and each dish was given to the person with the allotted raffle ticket. Knowing that the food would be raffled, imagine how I felt on one occasion when a large bluebottle buzzed around and landed in the sauce I was making for a roulade. I thought hard. No one in the audience seemed to be aware of the bluebottle up with me on the stage so I decided to let it die in the heat of the sauce, which was made with chopped mushrooms – one dead bluebottle might easily blend in with the small pieces of mushroom. The sauce would bubble and then be cooked with the eggs added, for the roulade. I still wonder who ate that mushroom roulade eventually . . . with its unintentional added protein.

One of the worst aspects of the Highland Show remains to this day, and it is something no one can alter – the weather. During the many years when the *Scotsman* cooking dems took place in the car auction hall, the roof was corrugated iron. One year when the weather was exceptionally hot, the temperature within the hall was so great that whenever I took a bowl of whipped cream from the fridge under the work surface on the stage it would collapse into a buttery slop before my and the audience's eyes. Hell couldn't have been hotter than the Highland Show that year. I spent my time trying not to look like a steamed suet pudding. When you are on a stage demonstrating food, I consider it of vital importance to look as un-repellent as possible. I had my work cut out that year. Other years have been as cold as that year was hot – teeth-chatteringly chilly. The vagaries of Scottish summer weather can never be underestimated.

During this decade, I began to be invited to do demonstrations for various charities up and down the country, as well as those on a business footing for which I was paid. I never asked a fee for fund-raising dems, which paid dividends in the following years when we started our shop at Kinloch because then – and we still have the same arrangement now – we ask the organisers if we can bring some of the contents of our shop with us to sell and cover our costs, which it more than does because we usually sell a great number of my books. In our shop, we also sell the Claire Macdonald range of jams, jellies and savoury sauces and the kitchen equipment that I use on dems – dishes, pots, pans and kitchen gadgets.

Early in our years at Kinloch, we were joined on the staff by Katherine Robertson. Big K, as she was affectionately known, came from Sleat and her father had been a gamekeeper on my father-in-law's estate but she grew up mostly in Glasgow, always returning to Skye for holidays and to catch up with her extended family. Her husband was from Skye too, from the nearby township of Drumfearn. Highly intelligent and a great character, she made wonderful fudge, shortbread, tomato chutney and scones and was a great part of our lives. We all love a bit of gossip and she was the source of lots – even if some was a bit improbable. When she arrived for work, if I was at the cooker as she walked past the window and if her chin was leading her body, I knew she was about to impart some 'news' and, when she duly did, she always started with 'Do you know this?' before going on to tell us of some local happening. The most memorable thing she told us was that a penguin had been seen in Drumfearn. To this day, I am sure she was right and, although I never saw it for myself, if Katherine said a penguin had been seen in Drumfearn, then it must have been so! She was an intensely proud and devoted mother to her two children, 'wee' John, who grew to be well over six feet tall, and daughter Catriona, and, later, she looked after her granddaughter 'wee' Mhairi much of the time. Mhairi went to the primary school with our girls and I loved her dearly.

Katherine travelled to and from her work in an ancient but much-cherished car. Husband John had the better car but hers was a veritable relic of the road – it lacked bits. One of the bits it lacked was most of the floor and one day, when she was driving Sionach MacInnes , one of the kitchen staff, back to her home in Drumfearn, she inadvertently drove over a large cowpat and poor Sionach was well and truly splattered, but, true to form, they both laughed as they related this next day.

Katherine worked at Kinloch in a variety of roles, helping us in the kitchen, helping Millie with the secretarial work, helping in the housekeeping department. Whatever she did she did well and yet she suffered – chiefly from painful phlebitis. She was always loathe to be off work and would often come to work when she should have stayed at home, probably in her bed. Godfrey and I were devastated when she died suddenly, aged only forty-seven. Godfrey has done so many things in our lives together which have made me feel very proud of him and not the least of these was the eulogy he gave at Katherine's funeral. He did her full justice and I know how happy he made her family feel, even in their grief.

The Birth of the League of Friends of the MacKinnon Memorial Hospital, Broadford

I can't remember exactly which year heralded my involvement with the then fledgling League of Friends of our excellent small hospital in Broadford or who it was who instigated it but I was asked to be their chairman and started to raise help, both financially and practically for the hospital. The secretary, Barbara Reytiens, had started Seathrift Croft Enterprise, the flower shop in Kyle of Lochalsh, and, before she and her husband divorced, they had run the Loch Duich Hotel, so she understood our way of life at Kinloch very well. The treasurer was John Kubale, a marvellous man who had worked for a bank, I think, but was, by then, retired and living down the Elgol road near Strathaird. The rest of the committee consisted of a splendid lot of people, one in particular becoming another friend, Elizabeth Macintosh, who lives near Torrin, also down the Elgol road. I feel that I must have appeared little short of a bumbling idiot in my role as chairman, crippled as I was before each meeting by acute nerves at having to speak even to such a warm and friendly group of people. They were all older than I was and each far more suited to being chairman than ever I became. We met either in the hospital itself or in the Broadford hall.

We started a tea and coffee service for the many clinics held during the week by the various consultants for which people travelled a considerable distance from all over Skye and from the more far-flung parts of the neighbouring mainland district of Lochalsh. We held annual Christmas Fairs in the hospital itself, which helps me pinpoint the League's beginning because I remember feeling terribly anxious as to how I could help at that year's fair while still feeding Meriel, recently born in the hospital.

With funds raised, we built a helipad below the hospital, which was of vital importance because, up till then, patients needing to be flown in by helicopter for emergency treatment, usually following a climbing or a road accident, had to be landed at the airport about four miles away, with subsequent transport to the hospital depending on whether one of the two ambulances was free or away on another call. As both frequently were away, the poor patient then often had a couple of hours to wait for transportation from helicopter to hospital.

After the helipad, the then surgeon in charge, John Ball (famous for removing virtually every gallbladder in the region), whose wife, Adrienne, was another friend, asked if the League of Friends would consider fund-raising to build a dayroom to free up the present one to give four more much-needed beds for the hospital. We all decided that of course we could and I suggested that one of the ways might be to gather together recipes to make a book – and I heard myself volunteering to take on the project. Not for nothing did Dr Johnson leave the word 'volunteer' out of his dictionary. I hadn't a clue what I was letting myself in for but decided that, in order to make pure profit from the sales, the cost of producing the book should be underwritten by selling advertisements. I seemed to spend much of each day on the telephone. I found printers in Stornoway, who quoted for printing the book, which I thought would be best done with a spiral spine so it could be opened flat – much easier for cooks when following the recipes. My first triumph was selling the back cover to Drambuie for £500. What a coup! I slept well that night – this was a quarter of the total cost of the book's production.

It's my experience that there are no more generous people in the world than those who live in Scotland, especially those in Skye and Lochalsh. Producing the book and raising funds for this building project proved my point and people also gave generously of their recipes. To my relief, these were more or less evenly divided between sweet and savoury, with a couple being for 'a happy family', which seemed to me rather twee but they were included nevertheless. Gradually the whole thing came together and we launched it at that year's Christmas Fair. To my utter glee, demand proved so great that, within a short time, we had to have it reprinted a second time.

The GP in Glenelg and his wife, Dr and Mrs Corrigan, held a succession of knit-ins, involving their whole isolated community, and raised a staggering amount of money for the fund. Finally we had enough money and a beautiful dayroom was built. It was opened by Prince Charles, whose helicopter landed on the helipad below the hospital – it was a thrilling a day for us all.

When Barbara Reyntiens became ill, John Ball operated on her and she came to us to convalesce. She was the most considerate of people and one of the very nicest. Godfrey and I loved having her with us for those few weeks and I enjoyed talking to her and listening to her balanced opinion of things, both local and further afield. We missed her sadly when she felt strong enough to move back to her home near Ardelve, overlooking Loch Duich. She had slept in Alexandra's bedroom (Alexandra by then was away during term times, boarding at Kilgraston, near Perth). Sadly, Barbara's recuperation was temporary and, within a very few months, she died, leaving her flower business to the people who worked with her there. She was a great loss as a friend and also to the League of Friends.

The League of Friends is still flourishing and last winter another cookbook was produced, which is contributing to the funds which are always needed to buy items ranging from furniture for the dayroom to medical equipment for the hospital. A hospital of the calibre of ours in Broadford is highly valued by the community and so it should be.

Memorable Members of Staff during Our Second Decade

Looking back, it seems comforting to remember some of the people who worked with us at Kinloch during our second decade in the hotel business. In those days, far too many considered that work in the tourism industry was what you did when you couldn't find anything else and that to work in a service industry was, somehow, demeaning. Now, as we are about to dip into the second recession within four years, with the service industry being the only booming industry in Britain, it is time everyone embraced the opportunity to work within it. Nothing is demeaning. Godfrey and I have worked in every aspect of our hotel, from cleaning out the septic tank on several occasions (Godfrey reeked of Jeyes Fluid for days afterwards) to cleaning out the loos, housekeeping, waitressing, washing down the kitchen and larder floors – you name it, we've done it. We have never asked any member of our staff to do anything, anything at all, that we haven't done ourselves and nor would we. There is nothing 'beneath' us – i.e. that we consider demeaning.

I received a job application from Sharon Dowie to come and cook with us at Kinloch and we arranged an interview in the Station Hotel in Perth, where I met her and her parents over a cup of coffee. She was shy, young and sweet and her references were excellent. She joined us in the kitchen at Kinloch and there began a friendship which continues whenever we see her. 'Wee Dowie', as Godfrey soon nicknamed her and which is how she is known to us both to this day, is a gifted cook. She has always been completely dependable and as well as all this she has a keen sense of humour. She is now the mother of Rosie and Neil and cooks at Sleat primary school – lucky indeed are the pupils there to eat Sharon's lunches.

Ian Smart came to work with us having previously been a member of the Highland Constabulary. When his son Scott was born, he went to visit his wife Morag and the new baby in hospital and there was a misunderstanding between him and his superiors, so he left the police force. In those days, he was able to do everything and with the utmost good humour and efficiency too. We relied on him for so many things – he worked behind the bar, he cooked breakfast on at least one morning each week and he was adept at mending things. Later on, some time after Morag became ill with multiple sclerosis, they decided to move to Portree.

During this time 'Gordini' came to work with us for several months. He was from Glasgow, a great character and also a great cartoonist – we have some of his sketches still. But he was unpredictable and he had his moments as a waiter, one of the most memorable being when he carried an ice bucket containing a bottle of champagne into the dining room from the kitchen. On approaching the table for which it was intended, the ice bucket and champagne slipped from his hand, hit the floor and the champagne somehow exploded, causing the entire dining room's occupants to stop talking as one. Undeterred, he announced to the stunned diners, 'Now wait and see what follows for my next act!' which immediately released the tension and defused the moment perfectly.

Gordini aspired to join the SAS and had set himself an exercise regimen which could alarm anyone who caught a glimpse of him, darting from bush to bush, with a seventy-pound load of logs strapped to his back. On a peaceful holiday at Kinloch, snoozing on a sofa by the window or out on a walk, the last thing one would expect to see is a man in army fatigues, bearing such a load, apparently evading pursuit. He had an endearing streak to him but sadly he had a strong addiction to drink and, eventually, he – or probably he and Godfrey – decided that he should return to Glasgow.

The Death of a Guest

I hardly dare say that in our nearly forty years of running Kinloch only two of our guests have died. Only! Oh dear, I hope I'm not tempting fate but that was the reaction of Angus Sutherland, the local undertaker, when I rang him one June morning in the mid-1980s. 'Is this your first death of a guest?' he asked and I realised, thankfully, how lucky we had been. I shall never forget that time during which, as well as the awfulness, I encountered all sorts of unexpected kindness from people – not least from Angus Sutherland himself.

Mr and Mrs B. L. had arrived three days earlier for a week's stay. They had separate bedrooms because he liked to smoke in his room and their two small dogs slept in his room with him. They were an extremely nice couple, in their mid-60s, who seemed to be enjoying their stay with us. Both looked well and fit – ever since this experience, if guests arrive looking ill, I fear the worst and am always grateful to see them safely down to breakfast.

Godfrey was away in Inverness at the monthly meeting of the

Health Board, of which he was a member, when, on their third evening, Mr B. L. asked for champagne before dinner. They were sitting by the fire in the small drawing room with no one else there when I took in the champagne, opened it and poured it for them. He began to extol the beauty and other virtues of his wife. She was embarrassed at his paeans of praise and kept telling him to shut up but he wouldn't – it seemed to be an outpouring of his pride in her and his appreciation of their lives together. He told me of trips they had made and asked me if I didn't agree with him that the new dress she was wearing that evening looked lovely on her. Of course I agreed and none of it seemed the least bit embarrassing, just immensely touching, although I daresay I would have felt as she did under the same circumstances. I left them to their champagne and they had dinner and eventually everyone went to bed.

Very early the next morning, I heard him walk past my bedroom door on his way downstairs to take his dogs out – he was very considerate and I had heard him doing the same each morning, walking as quietly as he could and whisper-calling his Jack Russells to follow him. Presently, I heard the three of them come back upstairs and return to his bedroom. I was getting dressed later when I heard Mrs B. L. call out in alarm. I dashed out and found her with her husband, back in his bed, looking very purple. It never occurred to me that he wasn't dead, which has always puzzled me. How could I have been so sure? Both of us were in utter shock, but I held her until we realised that we must do something. I rang our then GP and made the mistake of saying that I thought that one of our guests had died, which was perhaps a mistake because he took ages to come. Meanwhile I nipped to check on our children and told our mother's help, Wendy, what was happening and that she was to give them breakfast and take the girls to the top of the road for the school bus. I then went back to Mrs B. L. and she and I sat side by side on the other bed in her husband's room, looking at the sweet, considerate man lying there so tidily, as we waited . . . and waited . . . for the doctor to arrive, which he eventually did. He was not a caring man and, on this occasion, seemed even less so. He confirmed that Mr B. L. was dead and that he had a death certificate at his home and would fill it in and leave it under a stone at the end of the road. Mercifully, Mrs B. L. was in such shock that these details were left up to me. I asked what would happen to Mr B. L. and he told me he couldn't be taken to the hospital because, in order to be in their morgue, you had to die in the hospital. I protested and finally he gave in and arranged for the body to be collected by ambulance later that morning and taken to the hospital morgue after all, by which time I hoped that our other guests would have breakfasted and gone out for the day.

I took Mrs B. L. down to our kitchen/living room, where peace reigned as the children were now at school or, in Hugo's case, at nursery school. I made her tea, left her with her dogs and rang Godfrey to tell him what had happened. In an effort to lighten the situation, he said, 'I wonder who will pay their bill now, and they had champagne last night!' I put the phone down, disgusted, but he rang back immediately to say that he was only trying to lift the mood; impossible, it was simply awful. This was in no small part due to the fact that, during our interminable wait for the doctor, when I asked her if they had any family and how could I find them, she told me that neither she nor her husband had any living family at all. She told me that their great friends were the chairman of her husband's company and his wife but such was her shock that she could remember neither their name nor the name of the company. We seemed to be in a sort of limbo together, but she then said she'd like to take the dogs out for a walk so I nipped to the kitchen to write the menu and start cooking with Milly or Peter.

I shall never forget the part of that day's menu for which I was responsible – jugged hare with forcemeat balls, and pear and ginger mousse – because never in my life has anything seemed to take so long to make as did those dishes on the day Mr B. L. died. I remember dissolving the gelatine for the mousse repeatedly because, each time I was about to use it, I was called away and it set again. However, as the morning wore on, Mrs B. L.'s memory gradually returned. She remembered the name of their friends but not the telephone number – not surprisingly, poor woman. My affection for her and admiration for her spirit grew by the hour. At some point during that interminable day, I reminded her of her husband's eulogy to her the previous evening and the memory of what he had said seemed to give her great comfort. Meanwhile, detective work was underway to locate her friends via BT enquiries and eventually I got hold of the husband. He immediately arranged to get himself to Skye from Cornwall, by hiring a small plane, arriving at almost the same time as Godfrey returned from Inverness. A huge weight was lifted from my shoulders, as I was able to share the burden of poor Mrs B. L.'s grief with them, not to mention having help to make the necessary arrangements.

They left us three days later and we kept in touch for a long time afterwards. Not many years ago, I read of her death in the papers. She had been a widow for a long time and I often wonder how she adapted to her solitary life. She had confided in me that her husband had taken care of every arrangement in their lives – she didn't even know the name of their lawyer. With no children or any relatives, it seems impossible to imagine how anyone could endure the loneliness – but she did.

Mrs Dorothy Fletcher

I wonder if I'm the only person who sees a resemblance between some people and their cars and sometimes their dogs. One of our favourite guests, Dorothy Fletcher, who died during this decade, definitely shared a character with her small purple-and-black Citroën deux chevaux, with its huge headlamps. She would arrive at Kinloch at high speed, in a spray of gravel as she slammed her tiny foot on the brake, and you could be forgiven for thinking her car had no driver, because Mrs Fletcher was diminutive indeed and couldn't be seen above the steering wheel. Our children shared our love for her, their greatest thrill being an invitation to go for a drive in her car, usually issued very soon after her arrival from the Black Isle, where she lived, near Beauly, so she didn't have far to travel to get to us. I must admit to having my heart in my mouth whenever our three girls went whizzing off with her as she must have barely been able to see through the bottom inch of her windscreen, going so fast with her precious load, as she almost flew across the cattle grid, her wheels sending up sparks when in contact with the metal. My heart would remain in my mouth until their safe return.

Mrs Fletcher would stay for three or four days and was the guest of one's dreams, loudly praising all aspects of Kinloch to other guests. This could be slightly embarrassing as, on one occasion, when she turned to the table next to hers in the dining room and asked them if they didn't think that Godfrey was extremely handsome! They could hardly disagree for fear of hurting his feelings, as he stood between the tables blushing. Usually her comments were on the food or the furnishings or the service, all deemed by her to be of the very best so it was rather like having our personal PR officer in residence during her visits. That may sound insincere and she was anything but – just a very nice person whose appreciation was a huge encouragement for us. When Hugo was born, she gave him a silver snuffbox, still treasured by us all.

She may have resembled her small car in character but she bore no resemblance to her equally characterful dog, Charlie. Charlie was a Scottie dog loved by us all as much as we loved his mistress and Charlie knew his way to the kitchen. He was extremely polite, but he knew what he wanted and was never disappointed – his regular kitchen visits punctuated each day of their stay.

Oh, the heartbreak when we heard of Mrs Fletcher's death, which was not entirely unexpected due to her age – she was in her mid- to late 80s. Her beloved Charlie was taken in by some great friends who brought him to Kinloch on a visit, but he was truly a grieving dog and no amount of hugs or titbits of roast beef could assuage his obvious unhappiness. My abiding memory was of him sitting on the front doorstep, where he spent much of that visit, just looking at the sea loch and so obviously remembering and missing his mistress. We agreed with his new owners that they wouldn't bring him to Kinloch again. Neither they nor we could bear it.

Godfrey's sister, Janet, having worked in the School for the Deaf in Edinburgh, came home to Skye to live with their mother. We saw them regularly and, when the Brownies met in Ardvasar, Alexandra and Isabella used to go and have tea with them. It was a happy, peaceful life for them until my mother-in-law, Anne, was diagnosed with a secondary tumour on her brain. It was operated on in Aberdeen (by a surgeon with the apposite name of Mr Hope) and Godfrey and his siblings were told that she probably wouldn't live much more than another six months. The allotted time came and went and she gained strength. Although she never completely recovered and was always an invalid, she did get pleasure out of her life.

Years passed and suddenly it was time for Godfrey's and my fortieth birthdays which, because my mother-in-law seemed stable, we decided to celebrate with a holiday in St Lucia in the Caribbean. The doctor reassured us that it would be fine to go so off we went. Three days into our holiday, Janet rang to say that Godfrey's mother had suffered a severe relapse and that we should hurry home if we wanted to see her before she died. We made all the complicated arrangements, packed up and made our mercy dash back. We drove directly to Broadford Hospital, where we found the patient, sitting up in bed drinking a cup of tea. She took one look at us and said, 'But I didn't think you were due back for another ten days.' We didn't know whether to laugh or cry and, in fact, there were two compensations for our abbreviated holiday – the children were overjoyed to see us home so unexpectedly and, secretly, I was rather relieved because I have this deep terror of spiders. Just before we had had our summons home, Godfrey had been out for an early morning run and I went into the bathroom and found the largest spider I had ever seen in our basin. I stood petrified in the doorway until Godfrey got back, making sure it didn't move or escape. When he returned, he killed it with his toothbrush and even he was somewhat taken aback by its size. I was then terrified about the surviving relatives of our victim, which is why I was actually quite glad to be away from the place.

My mother-in-law finally died in July 1988.

Alcoholism

'Go on, have a glass of wine – just one won't hurt you!' has become the regular tease of my much-loved brother-in-law Anthony Milburn to my darling Godfrey, whenever we are all together. It has been the ongoing tease for the last twenty-one years, which is the length of time since Godfrey last drank any alcohol, following his nine-week stay at Farm Place to undergo treatment for his addiction.

There's no point beating about the bush – alcoholism is hell for the addict and for all around them, particularly their immediate family, but also for those others who love them. Watching the decline of an alcoholic is utterly soul destroying and there is no help to be found from the medical world, or at least there wasn't a couple of decades ago, and I'm pretty sure that not many GPs these days will suggest trying to cut out drink and replace it with visits to Alcoholics Anonymous unless they themselves are recovering alcoholics and know that this is the only way for most people to get sober and remain sober, with quality of life restored to the sufferer. And they do suffer. Alcoholism and all other forms of addiction are illnesses – physical, mental and spiritual illnesses.

Alcoholism is no respecter of person, gender or race – absolutely no one is immune. There are alcoholics in every profession – doctors, judges, members of parliament, as well as mothers and fathers and, tragically, children, the length and breadth of the United Kingdom, indeed, the whole world. But there is one common factor – apart from literally one person of my acquaintance, all alcoholics are extremely nice people.

It was during the winter of 1989 that I first realised that Godfrey didn't seem able to stop drinking and, as a result, could be extremely difficult, which was completely out of character. By March 1990, I had no idea what to do. Minty got another friend to ring me. A recovering alcoholic with Skye connections, he told me that Godfrey himself had to realise that he needed help and that I could never arrange to get help for him – he had to want to get help himself. Most of you will have heard the expression 'tough love'. Well, the spouse of an alcoholic has to exert tough love in order for the alcoholic to want to get better and to seek help. And get better they can, although this takes enormous courage and strength of will.

It came to the point when I had to tell Godfrey that I would leave him and take the children with me. The thing is, I didn't mean what I told him – or, at least, I don't think I did at the time I said it, but I could have, a bit further down the line, had he not sought help. My parents couldn't believe that he had such a problem but it only took one visit from them to see Godfrey drunk for them to realise that what I told them was no exaggeration. My wonderful father drove up to Skye and accompanied Godfrey to Inverness airport and then on the flight to Gatwick, where they were met by my cousin, Judith Coleridge, who is also one of my best friends. She drove them to Farm Place – con-veniently close to Gatwick. It was Maundy Thursday in April 1990. Farm Place told me that there must be no contact for a week following his arrival there. This was fine by me for, by then, I was drained from trying to talk to him, yet I pined to know that he was all right.

I had lots of distractions, however, as the Kinloch boiler blew up on Good Friday. Luckily, we had a charming guest who was an engineer who managed to restore it to sufficient working order that it would provide the house with hot water until the following week, after Easter, when the heating engineer could come to us from Inverness.

On the Easter Sunday, we had three members of staff from the girls' boarding school for lunch, with our then priest, whose guests the teachers were, at the priest's house in Dornie. Understandably, Alexandra, Isabella and Meriel weren't best pleased at having staff from their school there but Hugo was intrigued, especially as one of them was diminutive in stature and whose head was on the same level as that of our Scottish deerhound, Prudence. Following their departure after lunch, we had a good Easter egg hunt and it is a fact that chocolate soothes everything. I then had a wonderful surprise as a car sped round the corner and out stepped my mother, then aged seventy-five, having driven herself all the way from their home in the Lune Valley because Alexandra had telephoned her to say that she thought we could all benefit from a visit. This was light relief for me and wonderful for the girls, who were having a pretty miserable holiday so far, what with only me at home and the hotel taking up much of my time anyway. Welcome diversion, then, in the form of their indomitable grandmother.

When I took the girls back to school at the end of the holidays, I told the nuns, who were then in charge of Kilgraston, about Godfrey's treatment and how he was away from home for a few weeks. It is my experience that there are no more worldly people than most nuns and priests and I am thankful that they were still running Kilgraston during that time. Their understanding, concern and kindness were extremely soothing.

Sounding his usual self, Godfrey rang me the moment communication was permitted. He described his dormitory, which he shared with four others, and told me that he had been assigned a counsellor called Penny. He asked all about Kinloch and the children and was keen to get his treatment over so he could get back. I bet he was. Quite how the business survived with me at the helm I'll never understand – only just, it must be said. Until then I had never made out a bill, ever. I am completely hopeless at arithmetic and always have been – at school I didn't take maths O level but merely Proficiency of Arithmetic in which I achieved 13 per cent. So, for me, using a calculator is out of the question – I simply can't. Totting up the bills, remembering to write down everyone's drinks, etc. (which I frequently forgot) was a nightmare and I dread to think just how badly I handled this side of running the hotel during those weeks. Poor Godfrey. He knew exactly how limited I am in this most important aspect of our life and this must have been an added source of anxiety to him throughout his treatment.

We arranged for me to go down and see Farm Place for myself and meet Penny. Minty said she would fly down with me, for the day – what a friend! We got an early flight, which then served free brandy – darling Mint hates flying and had her tot of brandy and mine too, so, by the time we landed at around nine in the morning, she was very happy! My cousin Judith met us and the three of us drove to Farm Place. Mint was anxious that she might be kept there, as she felt that having had two slugs of brandy before eleven in the morning was possibly slightly excessive, so she went and found a bench beneath a tree in the beautiful garden and I went in to meet Penny.

It was very interesting, but I didn't like being greeted by other patients who seemed to know far more about me than I felt was warranted. I was entirely ignorant about treatment and recovery and I had a lot to learn. I read and read – there are many excellent books on the subject of addiction.

Godfrey worked his way from Step One, which took four long weeks, until he reached Step Twelve when he was deemed to be armed with sufficient information and self-awareness to return home, safe in the knowledge that he would have a sponsor in Skye and also that he could pick up the telephone at any time to talk to a counsellor at Farm Place.

I think that the two men – one a stockbroker, the other a doctor – who founded Alcoholics Anonymous sometime in the 1930s deserve far greater recognition than they ever get – apart, that is, from the fervent gratitude of recovering alcoholics and their families. Their form of treatment is thorough and, providing that meditation on their thoughts and findings are practised daily, the treatment is like insulin to a diabetic and all addicts can live life to the full in recovery. Attending AA meetings is a must. Initially Godfrey went to three a week, one in Broadford, one in Kyle and one in Dunvegan. Over time, this decreased and these days he will usually go to one meeting a week when we are at home but, if he misses several weeks, it doesn't bother him and he goes to the next meeting he can after we get back. They are an insurance policy – attending them provides the constant reminder that one is never cured, always potentially vulnerable.

During his absence at Farm Place, I found the attitude of people when they met me strange. It must be a bit the same if you are bereaved, as too often people avoid you because they don't know what to say. I suppose that alcoholism was an embarrassment. It was and often still is perceived to be a sign of weakness of character. (It is anything but.) To this day, there are people who will drop their voice and almost whisper to me, 'How is Godfrey?' I wonder what they expect me to say and it makes me giggle.

During his time at Farm Place, we were intensely grateful for the people who made the effort to visit him there – kind friends like Colin and April Strang Steel, Eliza Leslie-Melville, Isobel de l'Isle, to name but a few, and my sisters Milla and Liv. I think that if there is one thing above all we both learned during this time it is humility.

Following his return home, I had anxieties about him opening wine and generally being around drink but Penny, his counsellor, told him that her first-ever patient had been a publican from the East End of London and, as with Godfrey, he had to be able to handle alcohol because that was his work. He was advised, however, not to open champagne for a few weeks, until he was used to being home, because that is the only wine which, on opening, emits a boozy fragrance. Food can be as difficult as anything in a glass, especially with puddings when the alcohol isn't cooked out. For instance, kirsch with cherries in a mousse or as a filling for a chocolate meringue or cake, or brandy or orange liqueur in a chocolate pudding, or pear or apple brandy in anything. When alcohol simmers for a couple of minutes, the alcohol content vanishes but the taste remains so this isn't wise in large amounts either.

Godfrey is an inspiring example to many others and, after a few months, he was asked to make a documentary for Scottish Television, in which he would be interviewed by Edie Stark. I was dead against this because I hated the intrusion into such a personal aspect of our lives but it went ahead anyway. Godfrey was brilliant but I found it worse than I had anticipated. Neither of us had expected the aftermath – a daily postbag of thousands of letters, for many days, from people suffering the same illness of addiction. Some were from those in recovery who praised him for being so open and honest publically but the most important ones were those saying that they were motivated and encouraged, having seen the documentary, to get themselves into recovery. We tried to answer them all and I only hope we did. Those letters made my personal discomfort after the documentary shrink to almost nothing – it was only hurt pride, really, as I hadn't wanted people to see such intimate details of our family life.

There was one dreadful negative. *The Times* published a large article about the documentary with the heading 'Drunk as a Lord'. The interview had only been shown on television in Scotland yet the *Times'* article was published nationally. I was so angry that I rang the then editor, Peter Stothard, and protested vehemently, but of course, by then, it was too late. We felt so let down and hurt by such a derogatory article that we stopped taking *The Times*. Did they notice? I have to say that changing your regular newspaper is almost as difficult as changing your religion but, as I'm about to relate, I'd already done that. Eventually, we went back to *The Times* but, as I write, we are both thinking that *The Guardian* beckons so we might have another attempt, all these years later, at another change of newspaper.

Conversion to Catholicism

My change of religion had been gradual and the seeds were sown way back in my youth. I was reluctant to mention this milestone in my life because converts to whatever cause can often be fanatical and boring but, on reflection, it was such a major step that it can't be brushed under the carpet as if I was ashamed.

My sisters and I were brought up in the discipline of the Anglican Church, with our parents as our example. My mother not only kept a Bible on her bedside table, but she also read it regularly and, if one popped into their bedroom for a goodnight hug, my father would often be found on his knees saying his prayers before getting into bed. Sundays meant going to church. It was part of life and nothing prevented us from going unless we were in bed with a sufficiently high temperature to be deemed really ill by our stoical mother. Catholicism probably began to take root when we lived in Rome, that most Catholic of cities, and I was at a very impressionable age. We went to All Saints, the Anglican church in a small side street off the Via del Babuino. The second house we lived in was beside the exquisite little church of St Giovanni of Porta Latina, next door to the house of the Rosminian order. Secretary to the Father General was Father Ronald Catcheside who became a firm family friend, often calling in to see my parents and, during the school holidays, we three girls. We all loved and respected this wise, humorous priest and remained in letter-writing contact till he died.

Also close to us was Monsignor Gerald Tickle, Rector of the English College of Priests in Via Monserrato. During the summer months, we lived in the Villetta of the Palace above Lake Albano, which was divided into flats for members of the British Embassy to escape the stifling heat of the city. Directly below us was Palazzola, the summer residence of the English College of Priests, where we had a lot of fun attending the student priests' expert performances of the Gilbert and Sullivan operas they put on each summer. (We also enjoyed the delicious food, provided by the nuns who looked after the priests.) In those days, women weren't allowed into the Via Monserrato College, but I was only thirteen to fifteen and my sisters younger so we didn't count as women. Monsignor Tickle took us into this ancient, historic place where nowadays, with no gender restrictions, anyone can attend Mass.

We were all horrified when we heard on the news one day that a bomb had been sent to Monsignor Tickle at his Ennismore Gardens apartment, secreted inside a Bible. Next time he was staying with my parents, my mother asked him how he had detected the bomb in time to avoid detonating it. 'Well, Jeannie,' he said, 'it is a book with which I am fairly familiar and it just didn't look right.' He was always fun to be with. Though fond of them both, my mother was wary of both Father Catcheside and Monsignor Tickle. I think that the reason she had always been suspicious of Roman Catholics, despite the fact that they numbered so many amongst our family friends, was that she came from Huguenot stock so perhaps it was genetic.

Those two priests played a very important part in my life during our time in Rome. They talked to us girls as if each of us was an individual in our own right rather than just the daughter of friends. They even came several times to visit us at our strict boarding school. On one of these visits, Monsignor Tickle pulled a box of chocolates out of one of the deep pockets of his soutane and a £5 note for each of us out of another. I spent mine having my ears pierced at the jeweller's shop in Lancaster during the next holidays.

After we were married, Godfrey and I went to church on Sundays, usually at a Church of Scotland kirk in Broadford or in Kilmore, the local church for Sleat, built by Godfrey's ancestors.

Occasionally, we went to the Anglican church in Portree where I found the familiar words of the King James Bible and prayer book very soothing. Our local Free Church minister was a good friend but, when we attended his church for the funeral of someone we knew, I found the experience unsettling – it seemed to be instilling fear rather than hope.

Having been so close to Catholicism from such an early age, it wasn't surprising to find myself attracted. There is usually a catalyst, though I suspect by 1981 I was already halfway there and, for me, two events pushed me across the line. Our fourth child was born prematurely and didn't survive. He was never meant to – he had spina bifida and anencephaly, which meant that, where he should have had a brain, there was water instead. Losing a baby, even when not full term, cannot help but have a profound effect. Soon after this, Jo Wattie, the wife of the head-master of our local primary school, was killed in a car crash. She had been a good friend and her daughters, Eileen and Alison, were contemporaries and friends of Alexandra and Isabella. Her death rocked us all, but it was her funeral which made such an impact on me. Father Ronnie Walls took the service. He had been a Church of Scotland minister but converted to Catholicism after the death of his wife. He imbued Jo's funeral with a completely unexpected sense of hope which I found incredibly uplifting. That was the final step on my road to Damascus and, from then on, I was determined to become a Catholic. I wrote to Father Catche-side for advice and he found me the name of the nearest priest, at Dornie on the mainland. I rang him up and went to see him. Father Raymond Coyle was a small ex-merchant seaman, with a penchant for pipes – they cluttered every surface in his sitting room. Not having the luxury of a housekeeper, his kitchen sink was always filled with mugs and plates in need of washing up and his kitchen surfaces told me just what he had been eating for the days before my visits – open tins of this and that, the contents half consumed. He was a warm, welcoming man and I grew very fond of him. He was wary when I told him I wanted to become a Catholic. I told him that it was with Godfrey's full knowledge and approval but I made it clear that, if I was to be accepted into the Church, it was on the understanding that it was just me and not our children. I then started my instruction, usually preceded by a bit of washing up, over several months. My sponsor was Angela Fox and I was received into the Catholic Church at a small service with Angela, Godfrey and my father to support me.

I was so terrified of being thought to be fanatical that I went to the opposite extreme and my mother told me I was positively furtive. Godfrey took the children to the Church of Scotland for a while and then they started to come with me to the Catholic Church. Our girls went to Kilgraston and asked if they could be confirmed as Catholics, which they were, and, about fourteen years after my conversion, Godfrey decided that he would like to convert too, as did Hugo, then aged fourteen. They were confirmed by Archbishop Mario Conti at Mass one Easter Sunday, in the Broadford health centre waiting room, which was where Mass was always held for Catholics living in the south of Skye. Clarissa Dickson Wright was Godfrey's godmother and it was a momentous occasion followed by an excellent lunch – no great event is complete without a feast to celebrate.

Catholicism in Skye has changed completely. When I married Godfrey, there were about five Catholics on the island but these days there are hundreds. This is due to Catholics coming to live in Skye and also to numerous others like me who have converted, perhaps disenchanted with what they had before. There was always a small Catholic church in Portree, served by the parish priest in Dornie on the mainland, which is in the diocese of Aberdeen. Skye, in the diocese of Argyll and the Isles, is now a parish itself. There came to be so many Catholics that we built a beautiful new church in Portree and one in Broadford. About fifteen years ago the south Skye Catholics were lucky enough to be given a cow byre by Anthony and Jane Wilken who lived in Corry Lodge nearby. We all threw ourselves into fund-raising and, as always in rural, usually impoverished areas, generosity spilled out from all over the place. One of the events we organised was a dinner at the Dunollie Hotel with an auction after dinner which raised £15,000 just in that one evening. One of the items auctioned was a large clootie dumpling – a steamed pudding wrapped in a cloth – made by a member of the Free Church. This was what was so heart-warming about the whole enterprise – it brought support from all the churches in a truly ecumenical fashion.

There are wonderful clergymen from every denomination but there are also some who are indifferent, sometimes political, which can be uncomfortable and tends to make me cross. On the whole, however, I have found many deeply good men in the Catholic priesthood, including our parish priest in Dingwall, Father David Kay, who is a perfect example. As was Father Coyle, who once told me that he had nearly failed during his training in the seminary because his sermons weren't thought good enough, and yet I found his sermons excellent. He spoke from his heart and what he said was always significant and easy to understand, whereas I find some academic priests leave me none the wiser at the end of their sermons.

As a new Catholic, I found going to confession, now called the Sacrament of Reconciliation, extremely unnerving and, on the admittedly rare occasions when I go now, I still feel nervous. I try to prepare myself honestly beforehand and the compensation in the feeling of peace afterwards can never be underestimated. It is true to say that the Catholic faith is the core of my life.

The Bridge

During the early part of this decade, one late afternoon between Christmas and New Year, William Wattie, whose wife Jo was the catalyst for my conversion to Catholicism, arrived at Kinloch to pick up his girls who had been having tea and playing with ours and he told us that our bridge was at an odd angle. As I heard him calmly telling me, warning bells clanged in my head. Access over the bridge was then the only route in. It was just before New Year and the very next day we were due to fill up with guests. But they had to be able to get to us. This bridge crosses a small river halfway along our access road from the main road (then single track, now a smart two track highway). Without it, there was literally no way to get to or from Kinloch.

Immediately, Godfrey got on the telephone and the most amazing bridge-supporting, temporary-access-providing operation swung into action. Willy Sutherland arrived from Carbost with his assistant John-Alec. Willy is a legend in his own lifetime and has always been a valued friend of ours. With Godfrey helping him, he worked through the night and, within a few hours, the bridge was supported on a forty-gallon oil drum. It could have been pretty lethal and was not something the health and safety executive would recommend these days, but it made it possible for our guests to get to Kinloch the next day for New Year.

During a violent storm that day, the electricity ceased. Lachie Lowe, another good friend, who was in charge of the local Forestry Commission, appeared with a generator which let the boiler heat water and also gave us enough power in the kitchen to cook for our guests. I must say, we were challenged on all fronts that New Year but our guests seemed to enjoy, to a certain degree anyway, firelight to sit beside and candles for going upstairs and to light their rooms.

The Hydro Electricity workers are the most amazing team of men. We used to have frequent power cuts – still do, but not nearly as often – because when we have really strong winds the pylons bringing our electricity can get damaged and it would cost far too much to bury the lines, however much better that would be scenically. We often have hurricane-force winds, which never make the national news the way they would if they blew further south in Britain, but they do cause severe damage even so. Long before these intensely strong gales decrease, Hydro Board workers are up the poles and masts trying to locate the damage to be mended. We always know that when the power cuts out, it will be only for the minimum time necessary for them to do their repair work, even if this is days rather than hours. Living without power is a great leveller and absolutely maddening at the time, despite the romance of candlelight, yet somehow it does us no harm to be reminded of a force of nature about which we can do nothing.

Financially, being open for New Year is essential. Banks never comprehend that hotels lose money during the winter months and that it is during this slack period that any repair or decorating work must be done. One bank manager from Stirling who had very little knowledge of how a business actually runs once suggested to us that if we spread our decorating throughout the summer we could absorb the costs. Idiot man! That he had no imagination was obvious. How, did he suppose, would our guests enjoy the powerful smell of paint in their bedrooms and elsewhere throughout the hotel? The only thing to be done during these low-season months is to generate as much business as possible and we, along with many other hotels, have become adept at offering good deals to entice guests to stay with us during the winter. Back in that decade, we were only just beginning to get winter guests and Godfrey and I were determined to achieve having Kinloch open all the year round.

We had always maintained that Christmas was sacrosanct and we must be shut for that week so all the staff could be at home. These days however, such is the demand by guests that we are now open for Christmas as well as for New Year and the weeks before and afterwards. But, during that second decade, this was all in the future although we did occasionally, then as now, have one booking to take over the whole hotel and we enjoy this. It's usually for a special occasion like a birthday or anniversary and as we, as a family, love getting together, so we like embellishing such an event for our guests.

One such booking was for the wedding of the daughter of an Argyllshire family, who was marrying an Australian wine maker.

The wedding food mattered very much because the bride and groom were matching the ingredients to the wine served with each of the six courses, a different wine for each, including the cheese course, consisting of half a dozen of the bride's favourite cheeses. The wines began to arrive from Australia in an endless stack of cases but Kinloch isn't very large and we were soon having to find places to store it all, not to mention needing to get in more chill storage for the food. Godfrey had cases stacked in his office and I'm not sure that we didn't have some along the corridor to our and the children's bedrooms as we had to utilise every possible corner. And on the actual wedding day itself, I had my work cut out serving all the courses and finding somewhere to lay the plates as we put the food on them.

The planning had been enormous fun and I enjoyed doing the flowers and making the whole house look special but what none of us had anticipated, including, I'm sure, the families of the bride and groom, was how sticky it can be when families from opposite ends of the earth meet. Possibly, in this case, the fact that this was their very first meeting virtually on the eve of such a momentous occasion, which should have united both families, had a detrimental effect. Whatever the reason, it was extremely difficult and, although I felt it our duty to try to make sure that everyone had a really happy time, I didn't feel this was achieved. Possibly the father of the bride was unwise when he made a small speech at the end of each course and joked about the wines. He was very funny but the Australian contingent didn't think so – their wines were not to be the subject of jokes. Indeed, he seemed perfectly happy with everything we did for their great day, which was all that should have mattered to us but perhaps I minded that it didn't feel harmonious because, with three daughters of our own and marriages, hopefully, in the future, that atmosphere was not at all what I would have liked for us.

At the opposite end of the spectrum, around the same time we had another great family event when a Church of Scotland Minister took over Kinloch for his extended family for three days for a special birthday get-together. They were the most charming collection of people and I will never forget the sheer joy of having them and of feeling that they were all having such a good time just being together.

More Private Bathrooms and General Modernisation

Kinloch needed constant modernisation and upgrading and still does. During that second decade, Godfrey and I took a long hard look at our bedrooms and decided that we had to sacrifice some in order to make more private bathrooms. En suite was becoming ever more essential for the hotel guest then and, of course, it is unthinkable now not to have bedrooms and bathrooms en suite.

We had one room halfway up the front stairs which was a single bedroom and, oddly, although it was minute, guests sometimes requested this room. It had a window which looked across the small inner courtyard and it had its own wash basin but, to give an idea of its size, you could sit on the bed and clean your teeth at the same time – a compartment on a British Rail sleeper was spacious by comparison. We thought it should go and we turned it into a cupboard.

There were three rooms overlooking the pretty car-parking area with the sea loch beyond and we converted the small middle one to make two bathrooms, one for each of the rooms on either side. None of our bedrooms were large, the largest being on the ground floor, which has proved extremely useful for the less physically able, and we were now left with two, neither of which were ensuite, although each had its own allocated bathroom. Our tariff has always reflected the amenities of each bedroom – size, view and bathroom arrangements. This has meant that we have been able to have guests whose budget might not stretch to one of our better rooms but who want to come and experience the peace of Kinloch, enjoy our food and recharge their batteries –

which, after all, is the purpose of holidays whatever one's means.

In those days, the soaps, shampoos, etc. in bathrooms weren't considered the standard luxury items they are today, but we shopped around and, in line with my preference for local produce, I found a source of Highland-made soaps and shampoos for our guests' use. Sadly, that firm is no longer in business but there are several others in the Highlands, of which the Isle of Skye soaps are among the best. You can buy them by the slice so they keep their fragrance right to the last sliver but we can't use them for the guests because of their size.

Our upgraded bathroom arrangements, new curtains for the bedrooms, constant redecorating and refurbishment are all ongoing projects, earning us favourable write-ups from visiting journalists, which are a lifeline to our small business. You can never underestimate the power of a good article because, if people like what they read, they cut out the article and keep it in a drawer for use at a later date. We have guests who say they read about us in something written ten years ago and once we had a guest who showed us an article from an American Sunday newspaper twenty-two years old. We had no idea it had even been written, never mind printed. Sometimes you know when a journalist is staying and sometimes you haven't a clue until something appears in print, which can be a heart-stopping moment but usually results in a sigh of relief and gratitude at the end. Godfrey cuts out these articles and keeps them in a great file. We were staying in a hotel in Italy not long ago where they had numerous glowing articles depicting their success framed and hanging around the main rooms but we wouldn't go that far ourselves!

When King Hussein Came to Tea

When I heard the voice of one of my most favourite people, Michael Leonard, the former general manager of Inverlochy

Castle Hotel, on the telephone, I was delighted until he told me the reason for his call. King Hussein of Jordan and his wife Queen Noor were staying at Inverlochy and, later that day, they would be coming to Kinloch for tea with their entourage, who numbered eleven.

My dismay was due partly to the fact that, the following day, Godfrey and I were due to depart for the Clan Donald USA Annual General Meeting in Atlanta and partly because my mother had just rung to tell me that Alexandra had been admitted to hospital in Lancaster from her then school, St Anne's, in Windermere, with suspected appendicitis. I was not to worry, she assured me, because my father was at her bedside and he and my mother would cope with everything – hearing this was my greatest possible comfort, under the circumstances, and it meant I wouldn't have to abandon Godfrey on the eve of this big Clan trip.

Wondering who on earth the eleven-strong entourage could be, my next dilemma was how to get into the kitchen and knock up some scones and a cake in time for the tea. It would take them about two hours to drive from Inverlochy to Kinloch so I didn't have time on my side. My scones are not regarded as being world beaters – Godfrey always says that this is because I'm not a Scot – but that afternoon I made a passable batch, which is more than could be said of my cake. Why, on that day of all days, should I make a cake which sank so spectacularly as it cooled? There was no time to make another, so I'm afraid to say that I stuffed up the gap with vanilla buttercream. When filled and iced it didn't look too bad but it looked pretty alarming when sliced up and laid on the plates, with approximately three inches of buttercream propping up the top layer.

Because we were both on afternoon duty, we were busy answering the telephone and showing guests to their rooms, where we longed to lock them in so that we could have both the downstairs drawing rooms for the Jordanian invasion. Luckily for us, it was a beautiful day and the guests obligingly went for walks.

The royal party believed they were travelling incognito but you don't often see three stretch limousines with darkened windows on Skye. They were spotted as they turned off the main road and made their way slowly and majestically down towards Kinloch, so I had time to brush my hair and powder my nose, having checked that there were fresh soap and clean towels in the bathrooms and that everything was laid out for tea in both drawing rooms.

We greeted King Hussein, who was diminutive, and his exceptionally beautiful wife, Queen Noor. The eleven others consisted of security people plus two doctors because the Queen was expecting a baby so they thought that, to be on the safe side, they should have their own doctors with them on their travels around the Highlands. We took them into the large drawing room where we all had tea together. The conversation was much easier than I visualised and we both agreed afterwards on what a wonderful man King Hussein was. Against all odds, we very much enjoyed this brief Jordanian interlude and never have I seen, before or since, such spectacularly beautiful sapphire earrings as those worn by Queen Noor that afternoon. I cherished a brief hope that they might both drop off down the back of the sofa. As he left, King Hussein gave Godfrey several crisp new £50 notes to give to our staff.

The Festival of Food
and Farming, Hyde Park, 1989

The Highland Cattle Association approached me – or, to be strictly accurate, Mike Gibson, the well-known farmer and butcher, approached me on their behalf – to ask if I would do four demonstrations on each of the four days during the proposed Festival of Food and Farming which was to take place in the heart of London, in Hyde Park, early that June. Ever one for a challenge, I said, 'Yes, I'd love to,' but asked if Minty Dallmeyer, my trusty accomplice, could come too because it would be impossible without her. I realised that there would be virtually no time to buy the food for our intended recipes and prepare it once we were in London so methodical planning and detailed lists ruled our lives until our departure. Mike and his wife Sue couldn't have been more helpful and constructive, transporting much of my prepared foods as well as providing all the beef, in its various cuts, required for each recipe at each demonstration.

Minty and I flew down to London and stayed with Graham Beck, who had introduced Godfrey and me all those years ago and remains one of our best friends, in spite of him living in Cambridge and we in Skye. With really good friends, one just picks up where one left off, as we did during our stay with him in Shawfield Street, just off the Kings Road – extremely convenient. We were anxious that we wouldn't get a walk each day, just standing around doing our demonstrations at the festival, so we walked early each morning and at the end of each day but somehow pavement walks never really feel as if they count . . .

When we went to inspect the festival the day before it started, we noticed that the Highland cattle tent, with a large pen housing two Highland cows and their calves, was right beside the kitchen. At first, we thought, 'How sweet!' but, on further reflection, we wondered if this wasn't possibly rather insensitive as we were going to be cooking beef right next to them. We weren't the only ones to think this. The Animal Rights people thought so too and, for the first and hopefully the last time in my life, we found ourselves with police protection each day.

The dems went off well, as far as I can recall. We certainly engendered a great deal of interest in the unsurpassable beef from the Highland cattle, which are a gift to Scottish tourism because of their unique, endearing appearance with their long, shaggy, caramel-coloured coats and great horns. Not everyone knows that they also provide some of the best beef in the world.

The Festival of Food and Farming was an inspired way to bring rural life, with all its long-established methods of food production, right into the centre of the capital city of Britain. We were proud to be a part, however small, of such an event. Leg-aching it was but fascinating. The pigs, in their part of the park, almost had to be sent back to the farms whence they came because they refused to drink the London water. The weather was hot and those pigs really needed water yet they refused to drink. In the nick of time, a spring was discovered right under Harrods – where else! Quite how this was discovered and how the water was procured I never found out but the pigs approved. They drank – and remained till the end of the festival.

Home Life

During this decade, home life was busy. How could it be otherwise with four children growing up? Our three daughters went to Kilgraston. Alexandra had a better time there than her sisters, as it was still run by the Sacred Heart order of teaching nuns during her days. Isabella told us she wanted to leave and do her A levels elsewhere and she wrote to various schools without our help because, I am ashamed to say, we told her it was nonsense, intending her to stay on at Kilgraston. She persevered, however, and went to Loretto, on the outskirts of Edinburgh, for her final two years, where she flourished. The trouble with being a parent is that you have no dress rehearsal, no trial run. We assumed that, because we had three girls, they would do equally well at the same school and we were wrong.

Alexandra stayed at Kilgraston till she had finished schooling in 1991 and then went straight on to study nursing at the Royal Infirmary in Edinburgh. Luckily, she got in towards the end of the State Registered nursing training, as opposed to the diploma course, Project 2000, in which students went for months before laying a hand on a patient. She lived in the nurses' home – quite a revelation to her parents. I drove her to Edinburgh on 11 November to help her settle in. We left Skye in the teeth of a tremendous gale, driving rain and a power cut, with the water supply stopped, as often happened, by the sheer force of the storm. Poor Godfrey was juggling everything but we had to go in order for Alexandra to start her studies. She qualified as a nurse three years later and finally worked on the orthopaedic trauma ward, Ward 4 in the old Infirmary, which is now being turned into the vast Quartermile complex of modern apartments.

Isabella duly went to Loretto and loved it. She had inherited her mother's inability to excel at games and she succeeded in selling her games kit, unworn, at the end of her two years. She passed her three A levels and was offered a place at Hull University but to study a subject which really didn't mean much to her and we certainly didn't understand what it was about or what future it might offer her. So she did a secretarial course, went to Venice, Florence and Rome studying on a John Hall course, came home and got a job in Edinburgh with a firm of architects. Ultimately, she was PA to the Head of Communications at British Airways and her organisational skills coupled with her dogged hard work have stood her – and latterly Kinloch – in the very best stead up to the moment I write. (Isabella and her husband Tom moved up to work with us in 2003 and, later on, I'll talk about how they now run Kinloch, with a little help from us.)

Meriel began well at Kilgraston but, after her first year, things went steadily downhill scholastically. She became the class jester and, while not guilty of the drugs and drink type of problems, she was always in trouble by being just plain naughty. Godfrey and I were forever being summoned by the then headmistress and told of her misdemeanours which became, as it must have been for the staff, a pain in the neck. Ultimately, she was suspended for something of which she was not culpable – being such a marked girl, she was found guilty while, for once, being completely innocent. We took her away immediately.

She then went to Loretto. There was a change of headmaster during her first term and she was treated like a pariah by most of the teaching staff but there was an exceptional head of English who got the best out of her – as did any strict and worthwhile teacher. I attended the first parent–teacher meeting with my head held high, feeling that this new start could only be good and that I had nothing to fear. Wrong again! The first teacher was an elderly woman who glowered and pointed her finger at me as I approached and said, accusingly, 'So you are Meriel Macdonald's mother!' Apparently, Meriel had caused a boy in class to faint because she had, unbeknownst to us, acquired two mice, Mary and Martha, and had taken them out of her pocket during the lesson, hence the wimp fainting. I was summoned by the head-master and told in no uncertain terms that my daughter's behaviour didn't conform to the standards expected at Loretto. Something inside me snapped and I told him how sick I was at being dictated to by people to whom we paid a small fortune we could ill afford, and who seemed incapable of doing their job properly. I drove back down the drive in floods of tears, tears of helpless rage. How on earth and where would we finish her education?

At Basil Paterson College, as it turned out, and, having been nothing but a worry from an educational point of view, Meriel went on to Ballymaloe, learnt cooking as only Darina Allen could teach and sailed into work, where she excels right up to this day. For five years, she ran the events and catering at Euro RSCG in London, working extremely hard and with great success and professionalism.

Hugo, meanwhile, was at Sleat Primary and we had Annette Stephen as mother's help. She, her sister Wendy before her and the wonderful Alyson Hunter before them both were our three mother's helps, who exceeded all possible dreams while they lived and worked with us at Kinloch.

Hugo left his primary school when he was eight, to go to Belhaven Hill in the footsteps of his father, who had loved every minute of his time there. I felt my heart was being torn in two when Godfrey and I drove away the morning we left him at the start of his first term. We went to Holy Island for the day and had crab sandwiches for lunch and mine were soggy with my tears. Hugo worked hard, sang in the choir for the first three years, learnt to love not loathe rugby, acted in all the school plays and generally settled into school life as a boarder. The credit for all this must be given to dear Mrs C. The deputy headmaster was Mr Conran-Smith and Mrs C. was his exceptional wife who did everything. A marvellous trio was completed by the headmaster, Michael Osborne. All went well until his last year when everything fell apart for him and the whole school. He – Hugo – had been really ill with flu and had acted through the school play when ill. Afterwards, he was incarcerated in the sickroom and, from then on, he was such a hypochondriac through dread of being ill and having to be back in the sickroom, which, for some reason, he hated. At the same time, Mrs C. became ill with cancer. As was so typical of her, she was considerate right to the very last. She died during the autumn half-term. She had struggled on and it must have been terrible for all who worked with her and loved her so dearly. We, the parents, also felt her illness and death keenly. Hugo read a lesson at her memorial service, which coincided with Meriel's removal from Loretto.

The following September, he started at Eton, still following Godfrey's scholastic path and afterwards to Cambridge, where he read Arabic and Middle Eastern Studies. He'd actually been offered a place to read English but changed his mind before he went and managed to alter his course.

During this second decade, we had a Scottish deerhound, Prudence. A dog of great character, she was adored by all of us but not by the guests. She loved getting into the passenger seat of their cars if they had inadvertently left a door open, where she would sit with her front paws on the floor, waiting expectantly to be driven away. Guests were scared of her size, understandably, but she was as soft as butter by nature and they had nothing at all to be alarmed by. Sheep were another matter – she had no blood lust but she did love chasing them into the sea and not letting them out, by dancing around on the shore barking at them. Ultimately, if Prudence wasn't heard and a rescue effected soon enough, the poor sheep drowned. Prudence was beyond my control and Godfrey was in Farm Place and unable to help. On his return from treatment, things had become so bad that a decision had to be made. Coralie Fowler, who ran the local kennels, had a friend in Glasgow who lived beside a park nowhere near sheep, who badly wanted a Scottish deerhound. Prudence changed homes and adapted, we were informed, remarkably well. But the experience left me feeling rather a failure. During this time, we also had Florence, our first whippet, who was given to us by our friends, Colin and April Strang Steel. She was black and dearly loved and great grief overwhelmed us when she died, aged eleven.

Our dogs have always been a major part of family life – our 'children' say we always gave the dogs more attention than they received! Not true but it must be admitted that once, while on a long family walk to the Point of Sleat, we inadvertently walked between the cows and the township bull and, when the bull chased us, I picked up the dogs and ran. This has gone down in history not only because it is probably the only time I have ever run apart from during games of rounders, but also because it was the dogs I saved not the children. I contend to this day that each of them was well able to run themselves!

Recipes
from Our Second Decade

Herb Crêpes with Smoked
Trout Pâté and Cucumber Sauce

Serves 6

For the herb crêpes:

___

120 g (4 oz) plain flour
2 large eggs
300 ml (½ pint) milk
1 level tsp salt
15 or so grinds black pepper
50 g (2 oz) butter, melted
1 tbsp parsley, finely chopped
1 tbsp chives, snipped
15 g (½ oz) butter

___

Sieve the flour into a bowl and make a dent in the middle of the
flour. Break the eggs into this hollow and, stirring all the time
with a flat whisk, mix the eggs into the flour, at the same time
adding the milk. When all is mixed, stir briskly and add the salt
and pepper, the melted butter and the herbs. Leave the batter
to stand for at least 30 minutes before making the crêpes. To do
this, you need a non-stick crêpe/omelette pan. Stir the batter
well – this is essential after its rest. Put 15 g (½ oz) butter into
the pre-heated pan and pour in a small amount of batter,
tipping and tilting the hot pan as you do so to get an even thin
film of batter over the base of the pan. Cook for about half a
minute, then slip your fingers under the crêpe and flip it over
to cook on its other side. When it looks pale and slightly lacy,
slip the crêpe onto a plastic tray to cool. Repeat until all the
batter is used up. Only stack the crêpes when they have cooled.
When all the crêpes are made, cover them with a cloth or cling
film.

For the pâté:

4 smoked trout
375 g (12 oz) low-fat Philadelphia cream cheese
20 or so grinds black pepper
2 tbsp lemon juice
2 rounded tsp horseradish relish
small handful of parsley, stalks removed

Flake the flesh of the smoked trout from the skin and bones. It is worth taking time over this, removing as many tiny bones as you possibly can, as it will make the pâté so much better.

Put all of the ingredients into a food processor and whiz till smooth. The parsley flecks the pâté with green, which breaks up the otherwise beige appearance.

Spread half of each crêpe with pâté and roll up into a cigar shape. Put the rolled-up crêpes on to a serving plate or ashet.

For the cucumber sauce:

300 ml (½ pint) crème fraîche
150 ml (¼ pint) single cream
1 tsp salt
2 tsp lemon juice
1 cucumber

Mix together the crème fraîche and single cream and season with the salt and lemon juice.

Peel the cucumber using a potato peeler, cut it into chunks, split each chunk in half lengthways and scoop out the seeds from each half using a teaspoon. Chop the peeled and deseeded cucumber chunks into small, neat dice and stir them into the creamy textured sauce.

Pour the sauce into a bowl and serve to accompany the crêpes for your guests to help themselves.

Spinach, Lemon and Turmeric Soup
with Herb Scones

Serves 6

For the spinach, lemon and turmeric soup:

———

2 tbsp olive oil (in those days, I used sunflower oil)
2 onions, skinned and halved, then chopped
1 clove of garlic, skinned and chopped
2 tsp ground turmeric
220 g (8 oz) young spinach (in those days, I used thawed frozen leaf spinach)
1 lemon, juice and finely grated rind
900 ml (1½ pints) stock, chicken or vegetable
1 tsp salt
15 or so grinds black pepper

———

Heat the oil and fry the chopped onions, stirring occasionally, for about 5 minutes, or until they are soft and transparent. Then add the chopped garlic and the turmeric, stir for a few seconds then add the stock and grated lemon rind and juice. Simmer gently for about 5 minutes before adding the spinach, which will wilt immediately in the heat of the stock. Season with salt and black pepper and cook for just a minute, before taking the pan off the heat. Whiz the soup either in a blender or with a hand-held blender till smooth. Taste and add more seasoning if you think it is necessary.

These days I make this same soup but I add thawed frozen peas – about 220 g (8 oz) – to the ingredients.

For the herb scones:

375 g (12 oz) self-raising flour
1 level tsp salt
1 rounded tsp baking powder
1 large egg, beaten
1 tbsp sunflower oil
300 ml (½ pint) milk
2–3 rounded tbsp herbs, e.g. parsley, chives, dill, chervil, finely chopped

We often used to make small scones, either containing chopped fresh herbs – after Scotherbs started – or poppy seeds or grated cheese, to serve with a first course.

Sieve the dry ingredients into a bowl. Stir in the beaten egg, milk, oil and chopped herbs and mix well. This will be quite a sticky dough. Dust a work surface liberally with flour and tip the dough onto it. With your floured hands, press the dough to a thickness of about 2 cm (1 in). Cut with a small scone cutter and put the scones onto a non-stick baking tray. Bake in a hot oven, 450°F, 220°C or gas mark 7, for 12–15 minutes, after which they should be well risen and golden brown.

Serve warm with butter.

Potted Salmon with Lemon and Walnuts

Serves 6

———

175 g (6 oz) butter
1 level tsp salt
15 or so grinds black pepper
75 g (3 oz) walnuts, bashed into bits – I use the end of a rolling pin
375 g (12 oz) cooked salmon, flaked from skin and any bones – these days this is
    good made with hot-smoked salmon
2 lemons, grated rind of both and juice of one

———

I used to make this using up cold poached salmon – I am referring to the cooking method not the procurement.

Melt the butter in a wide-based saucepan. Pour off two thirds of the butter and add the salt and chopped or bashed walnuts to the remaining butter in the pan. Fry the walnuts, stirring from time to time, for about 5–7 minutes, then tip them onto a plate lined with 2 thicknesses of kitchen paper and cool them.

Put the salmon into a food processor. Add the grated lemon rind and the juice, season with the black pepper and whiz till fairly smooth. Briefly whiz in the cooled melted butter. Scrape the salmon mixture from the processor into a bowl and mix in the fried walnuts.

Divide the salmon and walnut mixture evenly between 6 small ramekins and smooth the surface of each.

Serve with warm toast.

Chicken and Broccoli in Mayonnaise Cream Sauce

Serves 6

For the chicken and broccoli:

———

1 chicken weighing 1.6 kg (3½ lb)
1 onion, cut in half but not peeled
2 carrots, washed and cut into large chunks
2 sticks of celery, washed and broken in half
1 tsp salt
20 or so grinds black pepper
750 g (1½ lbs) broccoli

———

People comment to this very day on this recipe. It has truly stood the test of time. Some of the ingredients sound a bit odd, I know, but have faith – it is a winner!

Put the chicken into a large saucepan and immerse in cold water. Add the other ingredients, apart from the broccoli but including the onion skin. With the water simmering gently, cook for about 1 hour. The flesh on the legs should be pulling away from the bones and, when you stick a knife into the deepest part of the bird, the juices should flow clear and not be at all pink-tinged. Cool the chicken in the liquid, then, when cooled, remove all the chicken meat from the bones, discarding the skin and any gristly bits. If you like, boil up the bones in the stock, simmering for a further couple of hours, and use for making soup.

Trim the broccoli into even-sized bits and steam till the tougher part of the stalks (which have the most flavour) only just resist being stabbed with a fork.

For the sauce:

———

50 g (2 oz) butter
50 g (2 oz) flour
1 rounded tbsp medium-strength curry powder
600 ml (1 pint) chicken stock from the liquid in the pan in which the chicken
    cooked
200 g (7 fl oz) evaporated milk
4 tbsp mayonnaise
2 tbsp lemon juice
50 g (2 oz) cheddar cheese, grated
2 packets of salt and pepper potato crisps, crushed to large crumbs, for scattering
    over the surface

———

Put the steamed broccoli over the base of a fairly large Pyrex
dish. Put the chicken meat over the broccoli.

Make the sauce by melting the butter in a large saucepan
and stirring in the flour and curry powder. Cook for a minute
before gradually adding the stock. Stirring continuously, add
the evaporated milk, lemon juice, mayonnaise and grated
cheese. Keep stirring until the sauce bubbles, then take the pan
off the heat. If you are intending to serve this immediately,
pour the hot sauce over the chicken and scatter the crushed
crisps over the top before putting the dish under a moderately
hot grill. If you are serving it later, cool the sauce before
spooning it over the chicken and covering the surface with the
crushed potato crisps. Bake in a moderately hot oven, 375 °F,
190 °C or gas mark 5, for 30 minutes or until the sauce bubbles
beneath the crushed crisps.

This dish freezes very well. Have no fear if you notice that
the sauce seems to have separated on thawing – it usually does
– but it all comes together on reheating.

Crab Cakes

Serves 6 as a main course, allowing 2 crab cakes per person

------

6 slices white bread cut from a baked loaf as opposed to a steamed sliced loaf
900 g (2 lbs) crabmeat, white and brown mixed for the best flavour
1 handful of parsley, tough stalks removed first
3 tbsp mayonnaise
2 rounded tsp Dijon mustard
1 tbsp Worcester sauce
75 g (3 oz) baked breadcrumbs for coating the crab cakes before frying
light oil, e.g. olive or sunflower, for frying

These are utterly delicious. They can be a first course or a main course but beware – crab is filling, which is why I think they are more suitable for a main course.

Whiz the bread in a food processor to form crumbs.

Mix together the breadcrumbs, crabmeat, parsley, mayonnaise, Dijon mustard and Worcester sauce thoroughly.

Put the coating breadcrumbs onto a dinner plate – the large size means less mess on the work surface.

Put two thicknesses of kitchen paper onto a wide, warmed dish.

Heat a small amount of oil in a large non-stick sauté pan.

Form the crab mixture into even-sized small balls, about the size of a golf ball, then flatten each with the palm of your hand. Press each crab cake in the breadcrumbs on the plate, first on one side and then the other, and carefully put them into the hot oil in the sauté pan. Don't be tempted to disturb the crab cakes once they are in the sauté pan. Leave them for a minute before carefully turning them over to fry on the other side for about a minute. Then, when the crumb coating is deeply golden brown, lift each out onto the kitchen paper.

These are good served with a home-made mayonnaise containing diced skinned tomatoes or with a sauce tartare – home-made, of course.

Casseroled Venison with Prunes and Pickled Walnuts

Serves 6

———

2 rounded tbsp plain flour

1 tsp salt

20 or so grinds black pepper

1.1 kg (2½ lbs) venison, weighed after the meat has been trimmed of any gristle
    or membrane and cut into even-sized chunks of about 2 cm (1 in)

3–4 tbsp olive oil

4 onions, skinned, halved and finely sliced

600 ml (1 pint) vegetable stock

300 ml (½ pint) red wine

12 prunes, stoned

1 jar of pickled walnuts, drained of their brine

———

Mix together the flour, salt and black pepper and then toss the
pieces of venison in this seasoned flour so that they are all well
coated with it.

Heat the olive oil – in those days, I would have used
sunflower oil – in a large casserole. Brown the seasoned and
floured venison pieces in small batches, browning the pieces of
meat on all sides and removing the meat, once browned, to a
warm dish. Then fry the finely sliced onions in the same pan,
stirring occasionally, for about 5 minutes. Gradually add the
stock and red wine, stirring until the liquid boils. Then return
the meat to the pan with the bubbling liquid. Add the prunes
and pickled walnuts. Make sure that the liquid is gently
bubbling before covering the casserole with its lid and cook on
a moderate heat, 350°F, 180°C or gas mark 4, for an hour.
Then take the casserole from the oven, cool and store for up to
2 days in the fridge. To reheat, put the casserole on top of the
cooker until the sauce gently bubbles, then re-cover with the
lid and cook in the same moderate temperature as for the
initial cooking, this time for 35–40 minutes. You could just
extend the cooking time on the day you begin making this and

serve it but it definitely improves when the flavours have been left to develop.

I have made this recipe since my earliest days of cooking at the Traverse Theatre, long before I married Godfrey. In those days, I made my first omelette when an order came in for five omelettes. Suffice to say that my fifth omelette was vastly better than my first. Talk about learning on the job! But this casserole was always a good combination of flavours and venison is such a good meat for casseroles or stews.

Gâteau Diane

Serves 8, possibly more

For the meringue:
———

4 large eggs, whites only
220 g (8 oz) caster sugar
sieved icing sugar and strips of baking parchment – used for decorating the cake
1 level tbsp instant coffee powder

———

Lay a sheet of baking parchment on a baking tray and mark 2 circles using a plate about 20 cm (8 in) in diameter as the template.

Whisk up the egg whites till stiff then, whisking all the time, add the caster sugar a spoonful at a time, whisking it all in. Lastly – and this is best done using a flat whisk – add the instant coffee powder, folding it briefly but thoroughly. Note that you can't use coffee granules for this – it must be powdered.

Divide the coffee meringue between the two marked circles and smooth it out until it's even. Bake in a cool oven, 200°F, 100°C or gas mark ¼, for 3 hours. Cool and then carefully lift both large meringues from the baking paper.

For the filling:
———

120 g (4 oz) dark chocolate, broken into bits
3 tbsp coffee – filter coffee or coffee brewed in a cafetière would be ideal
220 g (8 oz) unsalted butter
220 g (8 oz) sieved icing sugar
4 egg yolks

———

To make the filling, melt the chocolate with the coffee in a bowl over a saucepan of barely simmering water. Mix well and cool slightly. Then beat the butter, gradually adding the icing sugar, beating till the mixture is pale and fluffy. Beat in the egg yolks, one at a time and beating very well after adding each one. Mix the cooled chocolate and coffee into the butter, sugar and yolks mixture.

To assemble, put a small dab of this chocolate cream on the base of a serving plate to anchor the gateau and put one of the meringues on top of this. Spread some of the chocolate cream over the surface of the meringue then put the remaining meringue on top. Spread the rest of the chocolate buttercream over the surface and the sides of the meringue. Do this several hours before serving – it is then easier to slice.

To decorate, cut 2 cm (1 in) wide strips of baking parchment and lay them diagonally across the top of the gateau. Dust with sieved icing sugar and then carefully lift off the strips of paper, leaving a rather effective striped gateau. Yum! Note that meringue cakes are most easily cut using a sharp serrated knife.

This was one of our favourite puds on the menu for many years.

Gooseberry Cream Pie

Serves 6–8

For the pastry:

120 g (4 oz) butter, cut into bits and hard from the fridge
150 g (5 oz) plain flour
2 tbsp icing sugar
1 tsp vanilla extract

Whiz the above ingredients in a food processor until the
texture of fine crumbs. Press them firmly over the base and up
the sides of a flan dish measuring about 22cm (9 in) in diameter
and put this into the fridge for at least an hour. Take it from the
fridge and put it into a moderate oven, 350°F, 180°C or gas
mark 4, for about 20 minutes. The sides of the pastry will slip
down but have no fear, with a small metal spoon scrape and
press the pastry back into place and bake for a further few
minutes. Then cool the pastry.

For the filling:

2 large eggs, plus 1 large egg yolk, beaten together
300 ml (½ pint) double cream – you can use single if you prefer
75 g (3 oz) caster sugar
350 g (12 oz) gooseberries, topped and tailed
2 tbsp Demerara sugar, this is for scattering over the surface five minutes before
    cooking time is up

Mix together the beaten eggs and yolk with the cream and
caster sugar.

Strew the topped and tailed gooseberries over the base of
the cooled pastry. Pour the cream mixture over the gooseberries and bake in the same moderate temperature as for the
pastry baking. Check after about 30 minutes. The centre is the

last part to set and, at this point, it should barely wobble. It all depends on the gooseberries and what the weather was like when they were growing – hence the impossibility of being exact about how long this filling takes. If necessary, pop it in the oven for a bit longer. Once the just wobbly centre stage has been reached, scatter the Demerara sugar over the surface and put the tart back for a further five minutes' baking.

Serve it just warm. It really needs no garnish!

This is one of my much-loved puds and it works equally well when made with halved stoned plums instead of gooseberries. It was a favourite on the menu at Kinloch and is awfully good eaten cold when any is left over.

Pear and Ginger Mousse

Serves 6

---

300 ml (½ pint) double cream
1 tbsp ginger syrup from the preserving jar, plus 2 tbsp cold water
4 leaves gelatine, soaked in cold water for 10 minutes
4 large eggs, yolks separated from the whites
120 g (4 oz) caster sugar
8 pears, peeled, quartered and cored
6 pieces of preserved ginger, drained of syrup and sliced finely
a small handful toasted flaked almonds or a couple of squares coarsely grated
      dark chocolate, for garnishing

This was the pud I was making the day that dear Mr B. L. died. I must have dissolved the then powdered gelatine at least five times during the course of that dreadful day. But these days we use leaf gelatine. Before you start, whip the cream and chill it as this helps accelerate the gelatine setting.

Measure 1 tablespoon of the ginger syrup from the jar of preserved ginger into a small saucepan, add 2 tablespoons of cold water and heat. Lift the soaked gelatine leaves from the water, allowing any excess water to drip off before dropping them into the hot ginger water. Swirl the small saucepan and the gelatine will dissolve instantly. Leave to cool.

Beat the egg yolks, gradually adding the caster sugar until the mixture is very thick and pale. Beat in the cooled gelatine liquid, then fold in the chilled whipped cream.

Lay the pear quarters in the base of a wide and shallow glass or china dish.

With scrupulously clean whisks, whisk up the egg whites till stiff and then fold them quickly and thoroughly through the yolks mixture, adding the slivers of preserved ginger at the same time. Pour this over the pears and leave till set.

Scatter either the toasted flaked almonds or coarsely grated dark chocolate over the surface.

Part Three

Our Third Decade
1993–2003

Water Supply Problems Resolved – at Last

This decade encompassed several great leaps both in the business as well as within our family. We built and opened the South Lodge and Godfrey and I moved into it, with our bedroom on the middle floor. The Millennium, of course, came during this time, the planned festivities for which influenced how we would organise New Year from then onwards. This decade also saw the opening of the bridge from Kyle of Lochalsh to Kyleakin and, towards the end, Alexandra and Isabella were married within four months of each other, after which I considered setting myself up as a wedding planner. In between these momentous happenings, there were more of those swings between fun and desperation that are part of running a small business, especially a hotel.

By now, Kinloch had nineteen bedrooms, each with its own bathroom, some with a bath as well as a shower, some with a shower over the bath, some with two basins. Our dining room is very busy at lunchtime as well as for dinners, necessitating a daily mountain of tablecloths and napkins, and we are open twelve months of the year. I give these domestic details to illustrate how much water we use daily and how vital an adequate, reliable supply of water is to the running of Kinloch. We are still on our own supply. Our water is delicious – it makes water drunk anywhere else seem very dull – but sometimes, after a lot of rain, it is a peaty brown colour which, over many years, has always prompted guests to enquire anxiously if it is safe to drink.

This decade saw the resolving of our water supply problems, a nightmare subject which could well be a book in itself, together with the Bank of Scotland. You cannot run a hotel without water and Skye isn't exactly renowned for its droughts. The source for ours is deep within the hill behind the house, emerging into a small, deep pool about a mile up from Kinloch. It is tested regularly and has advanced considerably since Godfrey and I took over the running of Kinloch.

In 1972, it ran through a lead pipe 5 mm in diameter, which

had been laid in 1945. The lead was rotten in parts and in very hot weather tended to go soft and, in some places, even to melt. On these occasions, help was at hand in the form of 'Big John', the retired former Macdonald estates forester and a friend. (Incidentally, Big John's nephew, also John, came to practise as a dentist in Skye during the early 1990s. A brilliant dentist, he was one of the very first in Scotland to do implants. Godfrey was his first patient and now has more implants than his own teeth, entirely due to the skills of Big John's nephew.)

Big John's remedy to our pipe dramas was to bind the worn or melted patches of lead with pieces of old bicycle inner tube secured by thin wire. One of several problems was that when it rained heavily the force of water pushed the rose off the end of the pipe and the very fine gravel in the pool clogged up the pipe bearing the water down to the house. There we would be, surrounded by water with water deluging from the skies and nothing coming out of the taps. The guests were, understandably, mystified when we tried to explain on the frequent occasions when we ran out of water. Each time it happened, Godfrey had to go off up the hill, get into the pool and unblock the pipe. This could happen at any time of the day or night and, when it was dark, I used to worry that he might fall or that something might happen to him, so it was always a relief when he reappeared. Often during the summer months when the midges were bad, he would reappear *au poivre*, as it were – after being immersed in the pool, the midges stuck to him all over.

Deluging rain wasn't the only reason for our water supply ceasing. Over the mile or so between the pool and the water tank for Kinloch, the pipes were buried just below the surface – or, in some places, not buried at all – so day after day of hard frost could cause them to freeze. If the frost persisted, there was no alternative but to ask the Fire Brigade to fill the holding tank, which then took 2,000 gallons of water. For us, it was a case of frost meant cost but we had to have water, no matter the price.

As time passed, we realised that something had to be done.

Being connected to the mains water supply wasn't an option – we were too far from the main road and, anyway, the mains supply was not, in those days, as dependable as it is now. Thus began the ongoing saga of upgrading the Kinloch water supply. Our most important asset is the apparently limitless supply of spring water from deep inside the hill for which we are eternally grateful, but it became essential to get the pipes changed. In 1976, we replaced the lead ones with 2 cm-wide alkathene piping which was relatively new in those days. It still ran along the surface of the ground, meaning it froze in frosty weather, but, being alkathene, it could and often was blow-torched the entire length, which took hours and, if the frost endured for many days, blow-torching became impossible so the supply froze and back came the Fire Brigade to fill the holding tank.

In 1984, with the help of our friend Willie Sutherland, a contractor from Carbost, we were able to bury some of the pipe but only where it didn't run over rocks and these sections were wrapped thickly in an effort to insulate it. This was a vast improvement but some of the overground bits still tended to freeze in extremely cold weather. We then decided we must lay a completely new, buried pipe and that we must get a new holding tank. So, in 1996, Thomas Dallmeyer and Ruaraidh MacKinnon dug a trench at least 16 cm deep – a truly Herculean task which took almost two years to complete.

As a result of all this, we now have a 6 cm-wide pipe, properly buried and feeding a 4,000-gallon holding tank, with the water efficiently filtered, allowing our guests to enjoy our still slightly peaty brown pure spring water. They frequently remark on how delicious it tastes and how soft it is.

Rachel MacKinnon

Rachel was born in 1969, the year Godfrey and I got married. Four years older than Alexandra, she overlapped with her and

Isabella at primary school for only a couple of years and little did we know then how great a part she was to play later in our lives. At the beginning of our third decade, in the early 1990s, she left her job as secretary to Rob Macdonald Parker, the then director of the Clan Donald Lands Trust at Armadale, and came to us to work part-time as a receptionist and as a secretary to Godfrey. She'd married young and had a small boy, Robert, always known as Robbie, and a baby daughter, Vonnie, who used to come to work with her and be left in her carrycot at the end of our kitchen table.

There were no computers at Kinloch in those days and all our bookings were in the Reservations Book, which contained details of our whole working life. Rachel soon became invaluable and it was she who told Godfrey that there was far too much work for a part-timer and that she would, from then on, be full-time, which she has been ever since. No one is indispensible, they say, but there are exceptions and Rachel is one of them. She's such an integral part of Kinloch that returning guests always ask after her when booking; one of the most respected members of the Scottish tourist industry, the former managing director of Inverlochy Castle Hotel, Michael Leonard, a real professional in his field, used to say that she had the best telephone manner of anyone.

Rachel's family are a formidable clan. Her twin sister, Ina, lives up at the north end of Skye and their four brothers are all good friends of ours. One, Ruariadh, works with us at Kinloch now. They have another sister, Joanne, who is married to Assad Ahmed, the BBC newsreader whose wedding reception was held at Kinloch. Their much-loved parents, Roddy and Elsie, were the core of this remarkable family. When Roddy was being treated for the leukaemia which eventually took his life far too early, they gave a party in a hotel in Inverness for all the medical staff looking after him. He was admired and respected by everyone and was justifiably proud of all his children whom he ruled with a rod of iron.

When Rachel's marriage ended, it could have been awkward

because her first husband, David Smith, is our painter and decorator. Thanks to the diplomacy of each of them, however, it didn't disrupt our relationship with either. David is an excellent decorator, as was his father before him (who, incidentally, brought Alcoholics Anonymous to Skye). Eventually Rachel got married again, to the wonderful Neil Nicolson from Portree, where they lived for a short while, but she is very much a home bird and she missed her life in Aird, at the Point of Sleat, so they moved back to her house there, where they live to this day.

No one knows more about us as a family and as a business than Rachel yet, from day one, she has always been the soul of discretion. Her loyalty and efficiency are unrivalled. She is also great fun and eminently tease-able. She hates going away and Godfrey always teases her that the furthest she will go when on holiday will be to Harris, where her father came from, and he is usually right. Once, just before she was due to take a week's holiday, she came to work looking upset. Isabella, who loves her as a sister, asked what was wrong and it turned out that Neil had sweetly surprised her with tickets for a week in Tenerife and 'I don't want to go!' She emailed and texted Isabella throughout the week they spent there and she returned home vowing never to go away again to anywhere as hot!

Inevitably, technology had to come to Kinloch. Even Godfrey and I, dinosaurs as we are, realised that we must keep up with the times or perish. Rachel went on various courses and became far more proficient at the internet than either of us ever did but she could never pass on her knowledge to us – some people can teach and some can't and Rachel is one who can't. No matter how hard she tried to teach us, and it was quite probably our faults, we could never get the hang of computers. Of course it had to come in the end and it did, many years later, when our son-in-law Tom, Isabella's husband, managed to get us both reasonably competent at understanding how the internet works – well, Godfrey, anyway. I tap away on my laptop but if anything goes wrong I am lost.

The Skye Bridge

Rumours that there was to be a bridge built from Kyle of Lochalsh to Skye, just north of Kyleakin, became fact amid great controversy. All my years in Skye had been governed by the ferry. When leaving the island, we had to allow sufficient time for missing one ferry or, during the winter months when only one was in operation, for the inevitable delay should it have left Kyleakin as we approached. From the top of the hill beside Kyle House, you could see whether you'd catch the next one or have to wait. Coming back to Skye from the mainland, you could assess your wait from the hill above Kyle. The ferry stopped running around 11 p.m. so, if you missed the last one, you spent the night in the car park waiting for the first morning run around 5.30 a.m. This only happened to us once. We were returning from a week in Italy with my parents and we had Alexandra and Isabella with us in the car so those hours, yearning for home and bed, were interminable.

It might, therefore, sound surprising that news of a bridge wasn't universally welcome, but it certainly wasn't and for several reasons. In spite of the Inverness County Council's desire to have a bridge connecting Skye to the mainland, their ideas and suggestions had always been for an extension of the main trunk road linking not only Skye but also the Outer Islands – Lewis, Harris, the Uists and Benbecula – to the mainland. A toll bridge was never intended. Another reason for local objection to a bridge was understandably sentimental. Skye, after all, is an island of great renown and 'The Skye Boat Song' is one of Scotland's best-known songs; it was felt that the bridge would diminish its standing as an island, though there was still to be a ferry from Mallaig to Armadale. A further reason was economic. Frequently, one didn't have to pay for the ferry, awful though this may sound, because the ticket collector was a friend so, when it became apparent that we would be charged an exorbitantly high, index-linked toll, we all guessed, correctly as it turned out, that no one would be exempt from paying.

The reason for the toll was because it was to be the first privately funded road in the United Kingdom, the cost of which would be divided between the Bank of America and the German company responsible for the construction, in partnership with Miller Construction from Edinburgh. Quite why the government, then Conservative, decided to make such a remote section of Britain's main road system the forerunner for private enterprise is, for me, a complete mystery. The toll was a swingeing £5.80 each way during the summer months, dropping to £4.80 during the winter months, with only two days during the year when drivers were exempt from paying – Christmas Day and New Year's Day. For people who lived on the mainland but worked in Skye or the other way round, daily travel costs and therefore the cost of living shot up. The price of everything transported on to Skye from the mainland duly reflected the price of the tolls, not only for the Skye people but also for everyone in the Outer Isles. The bridge is part of the trunk road system up through Skye to the ferries to Harris and Lewis, in the north, and the Uists and Benbecula in the south. It was, politically, a disaster.

Among others to be blamed was the National Trust for Scotland. Colin Mackenzie, whose uncle had planted the wonderful gardens at Inverewe, had inherited his uncle's gardening genes and, in spite of having had lost a leg in the First World War (and going on to serve in the Special Operations Executive in the Second World War), he had created a garden at Kyle House of equal value to Scotland as Inverewe and bequeathed it to the National Trust. He believed they would act responsibly and, should the suspected site for a bridge, then only a rumour, need to cross his land, that they would refuse permission. He was wrong – the Trust capitulated immediately.

Our neighbour, the late Iain Noble, who had been a great bridge protester, found himself able to alter his opinion when he was invited to be chairman of the Bridge Organisation. I must state here that, although I was initially anti-bridge, we at Kinloch benefitted from the construction, not least because the representative for the Bank of America used to stay with us whenever he came to Skye on his frequent site visits and, on occasion, brought his family too. We became very fond of them as a family but he became understandably disillusioned by the ongoing opposition to the bridge and, once it was opened, he never returned, though we kept in touch for a few years.

Under construction, the bridge looked awful and I joined in the protests, but it was to no avail and the day dawned for it to be opened by Michael Forsyth, then Secretary of State for Scotland, in October 1997. The agreement was that, as soon as it was opened, the ferries must cease running, to ensure there would be no competition as that would have slowed down the recovery of the building costs and later, the profit, a fact that few people outside Skye and the adjacent mainland realised. We took to giving books of tickets for presents and for raffle prizes – the tolls on the Skye Bridge were far and away the most expensive for any bridge in Europe. However, I have to admit that, now it is finished, the bridge is beautiful, complementing the spectacular Cuillins beyond, and, now that the tolls have been abolished thanks to the SNP, we are truly grateful that we can cross back and forth at any hour of the day or night – a real benefit.

Suing Our Family Lawyers and Building the South Lodge

The heading for this chapter suggests two separate topics but they are inextricably linked. In 1990, Godfrey realised that the then family lawyers, Dundas and Wilson in Edinburgh, had mistakenly conveyed the ancient feudal Barony Title of Macdonald to Iain Noble when he bought the estate in 1972. This feudal barony was one of only three created after the demise of the Lordship of the Isles and, as such, was a very important part of family history. But Iain Noble refused to see that an unintentional mistake had been made. Furthermore, he began to seek a market for the title which, being a title associated with land tenure as opposed to a title of honour, held an enormous monetary value as well as being of historical importance. He advertised its potential sale internationally and had several interested enquiries, including a firm offer from a Japanese man, who came to Skye. We met him and liked him very much. He offered a million pounds for the title but Iain, thinking he could get more, prevaricated and eventually the Japanese businessman lost interest.

We put in a claim for professional negligence to the lawyers and, after four years of protracted negotiations, an out-of-court settlement in compensation was suggested. This was a small fraction of what the title was eventually sold for, around 2007, when it went for a seven-figure sum. We agreed to accept a derisory figure not daring to lose the court case on an unforeseen technicality.

It had become obvious from the early 1990s that Kinloch, as it was then operating, was only just viable. We were competing with the advent of 'boutique' hotels, owned by companies who appeared to have unlimited funds, and we realised that we must modernise and upgrade constantly and also that the business needed more bedrooms. Using the compensation settlement from the lawyers as seed money, we decided to build an extension. A guest, Larry Rolland, was an architect and he drew up plans for a house, but the basic design was conceived by the late David Roberts who, with his wife Marion, ran the Orbost Gallery. David was an artist, as is Marion, and we think their work is beautiful. David was an architectural historian too and he and Marion had restored almost all our pictures and portraits.

Our son Hugo was then a keen artist and he, too, loved the Roberts and had some input into the outward appearance of the new house, South Lodge. Initially, it provided five extra guest bedrooms, plus another three – one for us and the other two for our 'children' but they would become guests' bedrooms within a couple of years. Most importantly, there was a very large kitchen-cum-living room for us which doubled up as a demonstration kitchen and this has also been used as the large room for the hotel for all manner of events, from wedding receptions to parties of all types. There is also a fine drawing room for the guests, a downstairs loo and ample coat hanging space. One of the best features is the fireplace in the entrance hall, where a fire is lit virtually every day of the year, such is the weather in Skye. At Christmas and New Year we have a Christmas tree in this hall, as well as having one in the corner of the drawing room.

But back to the drawing board . . . Estimates for the building then went out to tender. The lowest was from a local builder, Calum MacKinnon from Elgol, whose initial enthusiasm matched my own. I was passionately keen to get everything right, but we were on an incredibly tight budget and I was well aware that the final cost must be as close as possible to the initial estimate. I decided on all the electric sockets and the door handles for each room, including the kitchen, and I wanted correct estimates for every last item, no matter how small.

Building finally commenced in September 1997, with a given finishing date of the following April. When it began, everything was chaotic. I had unfortunately come down with a streptococcal infection of the skin and my limbs bore a close resemblance to salami – completely hideous. I felt rotten and looked worse. Unfortunately, that autumn, *The Claire Macdonald Cookbook* was published and I was only able to play a small part in its publicity.

That same time, we also took possession of Plum, our beloved grey whippet, who was a sweet and earnest puppy, slightly insecure by nature but with the very nicest character. He joined our remaining whippet Tom, a rescue dog who was brain-damaged and never really knew his name. He was an endearing nightmare, who, within a few years, developed dog dementia which made life almost impossible because he wouldn't walk across any uncarpeted floor, barked to be lifted and then, when moved, forgot why he wanted to be where he was and barked to be repositioned yet again. If he was in the room now, during the time it has taken me to write about him and Plum I would have had to get up at least twice. No wonder everything took me so long to accomplish in those days.

The new house rose splendidly from its foundations and watching its progress was thrilling. Although we had been assured of April for its completion, Godfrey wisely left six further weeks for any bookings for it. As fast as the building progressed initially, it wouldn't be real life if nothing had gone wrong. The first and, as it turned out, major spanner in the works was when Calum the builder had an accident and broke his Achilles tendon, a most painful as well as immobilising injury. From then on, things started to go downhill and the building became slower and slower. Our first bookings for the new house were for 7 June and, if you run a hotel conscientiously, one of the prime rules is that any bookings taken are firm commitments made. Calum couldn't realise this but he wasn't a hotelier so we couldn't blame him. As the days whizzed past and we realised just how far behind the building work had fallen, urgent action was crucial if we were to meet our 7 June deadline, so Godfrey hired five extra joiners to help speed things up. I chose the paint, which would seem dated now but looked lovely then. We had dark red paper for the drawing room, with beautiful old-gold curtains and warm, deep yellow paper in the huge kitchen/living room.

It was important that the kitchen was an elegant room and didn't look too kitcheny. I designed a tapered chimneypiece to go above a four-door Aga. We put a handsome oak fireplace with a marble hearth and inner surround at the opposite end and had a floor of light oak – top-quality laminate – scattered with rugs. This room was created by the best kitchen designer in the United Kingdom, never mind Scotland – David Douglas, from Fife, whom I had first met when he and his partner did the kitchens for the Highland Show cooking dems and who had become a friend. He stained the elegant cupboards a subtle shade of blue and the surfaces are a blue-black granite, hugely expensive, so much so that poor Godfrey, when learning of the cost, went very silent and very pale. But the overall appearance was well worth it and I always maintain that the vast granite top for the central work surface can be recycled as the family grave covering – we could easily get at least six beneath it!

We furnished the bedrooms from Shapes, the excellent Edinburgh suppliers of antique as well as reproduction furniture. All our curtain material came from Cotton and Chintz, out towards Turnhouse near Edinburgh Airport, and was beautifully made up by Sue Ross-Stewart, the wife of the first cousin of my oldest friend Bridget Bowring.

We planned that the carpets should be laid as late as possible before the opening, so the week before 7 June saw me sweeping and washing out rooms with the carpet fitters hard on my heels. The weekend before we opened, our three greatest friends, Gavin and Minty Dallmeyer, and Henrietta Fergusson, who now owns the excellent Killiecrankie Hotel, came to stay and worked their socks off helping us to get the rooms ready. The furniture had to be unpacked and cleaned, the bedding unwrapped and the ensuing mountain of packaging disposed of, curtains and pictures hung, the beds made up and then the rooms cleaned yet again.

I had envisaged giving a drinks party the evening before the first guests came to stay, for all the other guests already staying in the old house but, when it came to that weekend, we were all so utterly knackered we could scarcely speak above a croak and we were almost on all fours going upstairs to bath and bed at the end of each of those days. Gavin was sleeping in one of the top-floor children's bedrooms in the new house, which was just as well because he discovered that the hot water came out of the cold taps and the cold from the hot – we would have been mortified to have learnt of this defect from a paying guest.

The 7th of June duly arrived and so did the expected guests and all seemed to be going very well. Godfrey and I moved ourselves over to our new bedroom, which took a bit of getting used to but we grew to love it. Our vast new living room, however, took longer to get used to. We had two large sofas beside the fireplace, with the telephone beside the Aga at the other end of the room so, whenever it rang, one of us would leap up and race the forty-five feet to answer it. We had a near fatal mishap with the Reservation Book one day. Inset into the enormous granite work surface is a four-ring electric hot plate for the cooking demonstrations, each of which is turned on by small horizontal fingers. One day Godfrey came in, flung down the Reservation Book and we sat down for our supper. As we ate we kept looking in the Aga ovens for whatever it was that I must have forgotten about that could be making the increasing smell of burning. Suddenly, one of us realised that the Reservation Book had knocked into one of the switches, turned on one of the hot plates and that it was gradually burning, right in front of us. In those pre-computer days, our entire business lay within these volumes so it was with indescribable relief that we seized up our slowly charring book, thankful that we hadn't left the room to the inevitable flames that would have followed the smouldering.

It took a bit of adjustment, living in the new house. It was nicknamed 'Whippets' Haven', not by Godfrey this time but by our stalwart friends, and the name has endured to this day. We had to cross the second car park to get to the back door into the old house and to Godfrey's office and, beyond, to the kitchen. Inevitably, guests would be arriving or departing and one couldn't just race past them, so a considerable amount of time was given over to chat. Added to this, our lives became more public than when we lived in the little part we'd built at the side of the old house, now referred to as the North Lodge. People would wander down the four steps into our living room and, of course, guests walking round the outside looked in – I would, too, though perhaps I wouldn't walk in with quite the abandon that some of them did. We put a small sign on the door saying 'private' but we might as well not have bothered. Around eleven o'clock one evening after work, Godfrey was 'watching' *Newsnight*, with his eyes closed and probably snoring, I having gone up to bed. He awoke to find four people sitting on the sofa opposite him, just looking at him. He recognised them as some of our guests because he had met them as he went round the dining room during dinner, as he did each evening, asking the guests if everything was good, if they had enjoyed their day, etc. Blearily, he redirected them to their own drawing room, which they must have passed to get to our living room, switched off the telly and came up to bed to tell me about his audience.

Although we had paid extra to have soundproofing, we could and did, on occasion, hear things we would rather not have heard. I was working at the kitchen end of our living room one summer evening with the windows wide open, as were the bedroom and bathroom ones directly above. Suddenly I became aware of the most dreadful noise of violent retching, which went on and on. Horror! What had the poor smitten guest eaten for dinner? I rushed to the Reservation Book to check who they were and to my overwhelming relief saw that they had been out for dinner in another establishment. The husband came downstairs to find help, the doctor was called, a calming injection given and throughout that night I was on alert in case I should be needed.

On another night, not long after we had gone to sleep, I woke up to hear my name being called. I rushed out of our bedroom and found an elderly lady, who was staying for our current cooking demonstrations, whose aged Labrador had had a stroke. I tried to ring the vet but couldn't get anyone so I made us tea and we sat up with the poor old dog for the rest of the night. During the course of those long hours, she told me her life story, which was one of such sorrow that I felt shocked that so many cruel burdens of misery could have been heaped on to one person. As dawn broke, the Labrador died peacefully. We wrapped him in his rug and Godfrey lifted him into her car in the morning and she drove away. I was doing that morning's demonstration so could see the sad departure through the window above the sink. We had offered to bury him at Kinloch but, understandably, she wanted to take him home and bury him there. The only tiny thing we could do to ease her misery was, of course, to give no bill. I often wonder what happened to her.

Above left. Claire with her mother, Jean Catlow, in Hong Kong, 1948

Above right. Claire with her sister Olivia, 1950

Left. Godfrey with his sister, Janet, at the front door of Kinloch, 1950

Above. Thomas Catlow, Claire's father, holding Olivia with Claire and Camilla, on leave from HMS *Ocean* during the Korean War for his father's funeral and Liv's christening

Right. Godfrey, aged twenty-one, in the grounds of Ostaig House

Claire and Godfrey on their wedding day, 14 June 1969, with bridesmaids
Joanna and Harriet Scaramella and Renée and Georgette Blake

Right. Claire and Godfrey, the day they opened Kinloch Lodge in 1972

Below. Claire and Godfrey at Stone Mountain Games, Georgia

Kinloch in the 1950s

The original dining room in 1972, with Godfrey's mother (front left) and Claire's father (centre)

KINLOCH LODGE

Tuesday, 21th April 1987

Garlicky Mushroom Soup
Fresh Crab with Tomato Mayonnaise

———

Apple & Horseradish Glazed Roast Loin of
    Pork with Prune, Cream & Red Wine Sauce
Baked Chicken with Parsley, Lemon & Garlic Sauce
Mousseline Potatoes
Glazed Julienne Parsnips
Cauliflower Italienne

———

Blackcurrant and Lemon Mousse
Extremely Rich Chocolate and Almond
    Cake with Cointreau and Cream

———

Fresh Fruit
Biscuits and Cheese

———

Coffee and Fudge in the Drawing Room

A sample dinner menu from 1987, handwritten by Katherine Robertson

kinloch
HOTEL & RESTAURANT

ENJOY A DELICIOUS COLLECTION OF MARCELLO'S SIGNATURE DISHES,
SHOWCASING THE FABULOUS PRODUCE WE HAVE AVAILABLE IN SCOTLAND

Slightly spicy pea soupcon
Wine Flight Z £32.00 (2 small glasses - 125mls each):
TAITTINGER BRUT RÉSERVE N.V.
BOLLINGER SPECIAL CUVEE N.V.

Steamed Mallaig cod,
caramelised grapefruit
Wine Flight Z as above

Roast quail, vegetable and Perthshire honey mousse,
cauliflower, port and orange jus
Wine Flight X £24.00 (2 small glasses - 125mls each):
CLOUDY BAY SAUVIGNON BLANC, MARLBOROUGH 2010 -
CAPE MENTELLE CHARDONNAY, MARGARET RIVER 2006

Slow roast Moray pork belly, seared west coast scallops,
sweet pickled fennel, oriental sauce
Wine Flight Y £28.00 (2 small glasses - 125mls each):
CLOUDY BAY PINOT NOIR, MARLBOROUGH 2008 -
NUMANTHIA, TORO 2007

Strathdon blue cheese,
prune and orange mousse, Perthshire honey jellies
Wine Flight Y as above

Rich dark chocolate espuma
Wine Flight ZZ £20.00 (2 at 50mls each):
VIN DE CONSTANCE, KLEIN CONSTANTIA, 2007-
NOBLE ROT SEMILLON, HENSCHKE, EDEN VALLEY 2008

Scottish rhubarb crumble
rhubarb ice cream
Wine Flight ZZ as above

Coffee and homemade petits fours,
served in the drawing rooms

Tasting menu - £75 per person (To be taken by everyone at the table)
£10 supplement for residents on a dinner bed and breakfast tariff

Wine flights are individually priced or why not share all four flights for £95

Kinloch Lodge, Sleat, Isle of Skye, Scotland IV43 8QY
t: 01471 833333 f: 01471 833277 e: reservations@kinloch-lodge.co.uk w: www.kinloch-lodge.co.uk
Registered Office: Kinloch Lodge, Sleat, Isle of Skye, Scotland IV43 8QY VAT no: 098 564352

A dinner menu from 2012

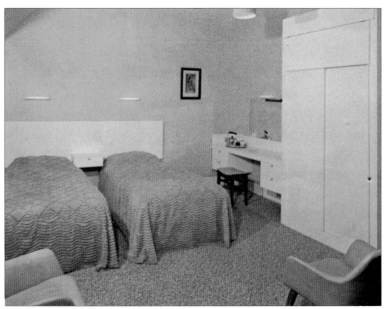

A new bedroom at Kinloch, 1973

A selection of brochures from previous decades

The 'small' drawing room and Talisker bar, 2012

The 'large' drawing room, 2012

Above. A bedroom at Kinloch, 2012

Right. The dining room, 2012

Kinloch, 2012

on Lewis and the prospective means to get the power from the Highlands to the Lowlands, though still not from the Islands to the Highlands. It remains to be seen if the Scottish Government is capable of joining the remaining dots within a timescale that will do any good for the Western Isles.

Gordon Ramsay's loss is Skye's gain

Gordon Ramsay's restaurant at Claridges in London loses its Michelin star. It is given instead to a hotel in Skye. That seems like a fair swap to us.

We commented recently that the long-term future of the Highland tourist industry lies not so much in grandiose marketing schemes, as in the quality of the amenities and hospitality we offer to visitors. That applies more than anywhere to our catering businesses. Right on cue, the Hebrides have won their first-ever Michelin star.

Quite apart from the quality of food there in 2010, there is an historical justice in the award going to Kinloch Lodge in Sleat. Other restaurants in Skye, not least in the Colbost area, have done an enormous amount in recent years to put the island on the good food map.

But Kinloch Lodge was first. Not so long ago, other Skye hotels dished up flash-frozen breaded cardboard fish, which had been caught and processed many months ago and hundreds of miles away, to tourists who could see out of the restaurant window the real thing, the delicious fresh produce being landed at Portree, Uig or Broadford pier — and then shipped off to Claridges in London.

Kinloch Lodge was the first to go the extra mile. In the 1970s, long before she became a celebrity chef herself, Claire Macdonald dedicated her restaurant in Sleat to serving beautifully-cooked fresh Highland produce. That has become the usual thing to do, but at the time it was pioneering. She set a standard. We who live locally might not be able to afford to taste the standard much more than once a year, but it has always been a regional asset.

Now her restaurant has won the Nobel Prize of catering. There are many awards available to hoteliers and restaurateurs, and these days many of our establishments deservedly win them. But the prize among prizes, from New York to Paris by way of Skye, is the Michelin star. Kinloch Lodge has joined an elite group which includes the Summer Isles in Achiltibuie and Inverlochy Castle in Fort William, but no restaurants at all in Glasgow. Winning or losing a Michelin star is a very big deal indeed. Just ask Gordon Ramsay.

The editorial which appeared in the *West Highland Free Press*, following the Michelin Star award

Claire giving a cookery demonstration for Quality Meat Scotland at the Taste of Grampian, Thainstone, June 2012

Above. Claire,
Godfrey, their four
children and some of
their grandchildren

Right. Claire and
Godfrey on the front
step at Kinloch, 2012
(Rosie Woodhouse,
Little People's
Portraits)

In the July after we opened the South Lodge, we gave a lunch and held an official opening. This was a splendid day and Isabella was home for the event, which was a great help. Clarissa Dickson Wright was staying as well as the Dallmeyers, Henrietta Fergusson and Brian Wilson – he who had founded the *West Highland Free Press* – who was then the Energy Minister at Westminster. Lord and Lady MacFarlane drove up from Glasgow and Michael Leonard came. Minty confused Lord MacFarlane with Michel Leonard and, on bidding farewell to him, said enthusiastically just how much she was looking forward to staying with him. He looked as puzzled as I felt. I asked Mint to tell me more about her invitation and it transpired that she had thought she was saying goodbye to Michael and was keenly anticipating a stay at Inverlochy.

The official opening was a great day and that evening we all sank down happily exhausted but, from then on, the new house had to pay for itself as well as contribute to the general upkeep of the business of Kinloch Lodge.

Demonstrations Abroad

During the early part of this decade, I received a communication, via my publishers, from the wife of the British Ambassador to Greece, Julia Myles. She wondered whether I would consider going to Athens to do two cooking demonstrations. She and her husband Oliver were organising two weeks of 'Britain in Greece', encompassing every aspect of life imaginable, and they wanted me to be the food interest. Of course I said I would go but that I would need to bring Minty Dallmeyer with me, a request which was immediately accepted. Thereafter Julia and I communicated by fax with messages winging back and forth between Athens and Skye several times a day until we actually went, in September 1995. I had no idea whether there would be shops close by or what foods would be accessible, so I decided that, with mammoth planning,

I should take virtually everything with me, with much of each recipe ready prepared. We were to stay at the official residence, where the chef, who was from Yorkshire, would have ample chill space cleared for all my requirements.

The day dawned for our departure and even our transportation excited me – Club Class on Olympic Airways. But Minty, who was then also working as a travel consultant, tried to dampen my expectations, explaining that Olympic Airways was not quite the same as BA. This was an understatement, as we quickly discovered. By the time we boarded our flight, our arms had lengthened considerably as each of us was carrying heavy chill bags crammed full of neatly packaged dishes containing the prepared foods and items for the six recipes we would be demonstrating each day. On being shown to our seats in Club Class, we found we were its only passengers and there was a notice on the back of the seats in front of us from the chairman of Olympic Airways telling us that, due to financial strictures, no new planes had been bought for twenty-five years. With this information, and then seeing a half-drawn curtain with the other half hanging off its rail and our stewardess sitting with her feet up, puffing away at a cigarette, I began to feel more than slightly nervous.

We had had a very early start to our day, with no time for anything to eat, and were both ravenous and could hardly wait for lunch during the flight. However, my expectations of a Club Class gastronomic experience fell way short of anything I had anticipated. After take-off, the stewardess produced a menu offering us two options for a main course – meat or fish. When I asked her what type of fish it was, she shrugged and said, 'Just feesh.' It was completely inedible, despite our hunger. Something made us choose to drink Amaretto, never before tried by either of us, and we fuelled ourselves with this, but we went down the steps from the plane on arrival in Athens stone-cold sober. I could never quite work out how.

On arrival at the Residence, a lovely house, it was great to meet Julia Myles, who was every bit as nice in person as on fax. I did have an embarrassing moment with her, though, when, at the start of my demonstration the following morning, I described Julia as 'my new fax friend' and she called out, 'I'm not that fat!'

Also staying for the two weeks was the artist Bob Brown, whom Minty and I loved and whose portrait of us both doing the dems I bought some months later. Also participating in the Festival of Britain in Greece while we were there was the crime writer P. D. James, whom I revere. I heard her talk at the Charleston Festival in 2011, aged ninety-one, and she was every bit as sparky and interesting as she had been when we were lucky enough to spend time with her in Athens. There was also a fascinating professor of classics from Oxford who wore wonderfully garish socks and an eminent thoracic surgeon who was demonstrating how operations could be performed on a patient in one country via a telephone link in another. Not very reliable, I have to say, if they were dependent on the British Telecom experience that has always been our communications nightmare in Skye. There was a group of musicians called Stomp, who performed in the Parthenon, making their terrific music on instruments such as dustbin lids, broom handles, boxes of matches and all manner of other household utensils. They were brilliant. There was a red double-decker bus from London, beer and many other aspects of all that is good about life in Britain. The whole festival was a credit to the Myles for organising and putting together such a spectacular.

When deciding what recipes to demonstrate, I had looked into the links between Scotland and Greece and discovered that there were many, including bagpipes, St Andrew, who is the patron saint of both Greece and Scotland, and haggis, said by some to have originated in Greece not Scotland, goats' cheese, venison and redcurrants – although the redcurrants almost caused a minor diplomatic incident. This was because we had been cautioned on arrival not to mention Macedonia but, during our first demonstration, a member of the audience informed me that most of the redcurrants grow in Macedonia and I froze, briefly, with the fear of possible diplomatic eviction.

The dems took place in the imposing entrance hall of the Residence, where long trestle tables covered with white cloths had been arranged for us, along with a two-ring gas hot plate. When we switched on the gas on our first morning, luckily before anyone arrived, flames shot at least four feet high, almost taking with them the recipe sheets and my eyebrows. We managed to temper the enthusiasm of Greek gas and we discovered that behind us was a fairly wide ledge with the air-conditioning grill inside, which was perfect for fast-cooling gelatine in stock, necessary for one of our recipes. I have to confess that we did inadvertently tip the contents of one lot of gelatine stock down inside the air-conditioning unit, luckily before the dem began on one of the two mornings. I often wondered, afterwards, if it began to smell a bit once the need for air conditioning ended and central heating took over.

The guests arrived for the first dem and they were indeed an elegant lot. There was so much Escada braid on their clothes, not to mention amazing jewels, many so huge that their wearers found it difficult to raise their hands very far or to bend their knuckles. As the demonstration went on, I became aware of the murmur of someone talking quietly but continually. This bothered me a bit until Minty whispered that it was a simultaneous translator for the benefit of all those who didn't speak English. During the dem that day and the next, I tried to include as much information about Scotland as I could, seeing it as an opportunity to extol its beauty as well as its wonderful food.

The extensive kitchens for the Residence were in the basement, with three walk-in chill rooms, one entirely given over to us. The weather was so hot that Minty and I would go and sit in our chill room for five minutes from time to time, to cool down. The chef, who had his own sitting room near the kitchen, was charming but was, I felt, on a pretty easy wicket, as he only did dinner on alternate nights and we went out for dinner on the others. In all, it was a fascinating experience for both of us, if completely exhausting.

In 1996, I was invited to demonstrate in New York, at Macy's store, because Scotland the Brand was taking over New York City for a few days, filling every shop window with Scottish goods. Godfrey and I had returned from visiting Alexandra, who was living and working in Hong Kong, and I had a 48-hour turnaround before leaving for New York, loaded yet again with chill bags containing masses of frozen prepared foods and dishes for my two dems. All this would have been quite impossible a decade later, what with the one piece of hand luggage permitted on a flight, not to mention the total ban on all fluids. I took with me frozen herb crêpe batter as one of my food items, as well as smoked salmon and countless other things, all essential because of the lack of time or kitchen space to do any preparation when I got there. For this trip, though, I struck gold. Our friend Henrietta Fergusson, who had lived in New York for a year some time previously, was then working for a consortium of Americans, all very keen golfers, who owned a house in Gullane which was run and organised by Henrietta. She had been lent an apartment (although I don't remember that it had a kitchen) and was going to be in New York when the Scotland the Brand trip was on. She asked me to stay – there was a sofa bed – and a trip which, on my own, could have been fraught with dread turned into being huge fun. I had spent time in New York on several previous occasions and I love the city, as does Hen. We managed to fit in visits to the Metropolitan Museum, where there was a Fabergé exhibition, as well as visits to food shops, on top of all the official Scotland the Brand events we had to attend. One of these stands out in my memory – a dinner given for all of us attending by Robert Forbes, in the Forbes Galleries on 12th Street, where they have more Fabergé, as well as all sorts of other fascinating memorabilia. The dinner was splendid, too.

On the day I was due to fly home, Henrietta and I met Helen MacDonald, who is married to Mac – Nester MacDonald – for lunch in the Plaza Hotel. We had stayed with them often at both their New Jersey home and in North Carolina, in Linville, where Mac had been one of the founders of the great Grandfather Mountain Highland Games. He was one of our very first contributors to the Clan Donald Lands Trust and he and Helen, although very much older than us, became two of our favourite American Macdonalds. They were a truly devoted couple and great fun to be with, making us laugh and laugh. We had a splendid lunch together but that afternoon there came the appalling news of the massacre in Dunblane. I flew home, via Manchester, where I bought newspapers to read on the flight to Edinburgh and they were full of all the horror of the previous day's shootings. I then got into the car and drove as far as Blair Atholl, where the road was closed because of snow. Almost at the end of my tether, I turned round, cut across and went up the A82, through Glencoe and up via Fort William, eventually getting to the bridge and back to Kinloch, thankful to be safely back home with Godfrey.

Another American cooking demonstration took place in North Carolina a couple of years later. Godfrey and I, with Hugo, whom we thought might benefit from an early indoctrination into Clan Donald life, were guests of Mac and Helen in their beautiful and comfortable house at Linville. Helen was a prolific artist and she and Hugo struck up a great friendship – he, who loved drawing and painting, was a great admirer of her work. We were there to be what is called Honoured Guests at the Grandfather Mountain Highland Games, which take place up the mountain from Linville on a wide, natural plateau. The only drawback to these Games is the access road – there is only one way in and out and usually, or in those days anyway, upwards of 70,000 people attended the four-day event, many of them camping out near the Games fields.

Helen had asked if I would do a cooking demonstration on a morning before the Games began, which she organised. I forget what the ticket sale proceeds were in aid of but it was a local charity of which she was the patron. I brought most things with me and, when everyone was seated, I began the dem. One of the ingredients I was using was finely diced garlic, its flavour preserved in olive oil – air taints the flavour of any member of the onion family and garlic is no exception. As I described this fact to the assembled company, one woman called out, 'But isn't there a risk of botulism if you put garlic in olive oil?' The very mention of the word 'botulism', surely the most deadly of all bacteria, caused everyone to gasp. From then on, nothing I said or did held any credence whatsoever for those present. The rest of the demonstration had been killed stone dead and I could happily have administered a large dose of botulism to the woman who spoke out as she did.

I did one other cooking dem in New York, but this time quite alone. The flight out was a nightmare enshrined in family lore. I sat next to an elderly lady and in the seat directly in front of us was a little girl who seemed to be sick throughout much of the journey. The stewardesses were in constant attendance but when my elderly neighbour rang the bell to ask for assistance in getting to the loo, they asked if I would take her. I did and have no wish to dwell on that but, as we returned to our seats, I began to realise that all was not quite right with my seat companion, who seemed to have become my sole responsibility. She had severe dementia and, for the next six hours, she said the same thing to me so frequently that I lost count. 'Have you heard of Lord Byron? Well, my son lives in the same village as he did.' I tried shutting my eyes and feigning sleep but to no avail. On and on she went – 'Have you heard of Lord Byron? Well, my son lives in the same village as he did.' I thought I would go mad. It couldn't have felt longer had I flown to Australia but eventually we landed in JFK airport. 'And then what?' I wondered. Was I doomed to spend the rest of my life with this poor, dotty old lady? I had, amongst my hand luggage, a container of meringues, I remember, and was terrified of breaking them. She and I shuffled through immigration and retrieved our luggage and, to my huge relief, she was met by her daughter. I handed her over, longing to say that she really should never have travelled by herself. But I didn't – I was so weak with relief to see the last of her. The rest of that brief trip pales into nothing in my memory, apart from the fact that it was the first time I was given a card to open my hotel room door as opposed to a key to lock and unlock.

Being invited to do demonstrations in far-off lands is very different to when we can just load up the van with all the stuff we need and drive off with it; instead, it means meticulous planning and lists. The recipes for such dems are entirely dictated by the practicality and transportability of various foodstuffs. So many are perishable under most travel conditions whereas others travel well, with careful wrapping – eggs, for instance, if carefully packed within something else, are easy. Foods that are time consuming to prepare immediately before a dem, but which can be done in advance and even frozen, are diced or sliced onions, fried and cooled before being packaged. Labelling saves enor-mous time when assembling everything for each recipe. This may all sound pedantic but it's how I work and it would seem impossible to me without such organisation.

Although air travel these days is such hell, with passengers restricted to one regulation-size bag per person for hand luggage, travelling alone in those days presented other imponderables and many times I yearned to possess at least one more arm and hand. I reckon I'm pretty impressive in just how much I can carry and, on more than one occasion, were they stronger, I would even have resorted to carrying a bag in my teeth.

One last solo excursion abroad came my way during this decade, following the publication of my book *The Harrods Book of Entertaining*. I was invited to speak about 'Food in Scotland' at the Wadsworth Atheneum Museum, in Hartford, Connecticut, one May. I flew out and stayed a couple of nights with my American Aunt Janie and Uncle Tony, my father's younger brother. They then drove me to Hartford, where I stayed as a guest of one of the Junior League members who were organising the event. The evening before my talk there was a reception, in the Atheneum, so at least I had a glimpse of where I would be performing the following day. As is my wont before something as momentous, I scarcely slept a wink and was up very early, to wash my hair and gather my thoughts, quietly rehearsing what I was going to say. My mother once told me that, because time never stands still and always moves forward, nothing, however dreaded, lasts for ever. I have hugged this comforting thought on many occasions and this was one of them. It's almost worth doing something really terrifying because of the jubilant relief when it is safely over. My talk ended, after which the Q and A session seemed a breeze and then there was nothing left to be afraid of, only going home to look forward to.

The Missing Guest

Early in this decade, one late September Saturday, we had Alexandra and Isabella home for the weekend from Kilgraston. At about seven that evening, I was in the entrance hall when I saw one of our guests hovering. She told me that she was worried about her husband, who had gone for a brief walk an hour earlier and, as it was getting on for dinner time, which in those days we served at 8 p.m., she couldn't understand why he hadn't returned. I tried to reassure her and went to find Godfrey, who immediately said that he would take a torch and go up the forestry track behind Kinloch to look for him, expecting that perhaps he had twisted his ankle or something. I took the wife into our sitting room – this was before Whippets' Haven was built – and the girls tactfully removed themselves to our kitchen.

Godfrey returned, having seen no sign of him, and decided that we must call out the police and a search party. In a short time, the wife and I found ourselves in the company of two policemen, who asked her all sorts of questions from which I learned that her husband was a GP, that he was extremely fit, a hill-walker, and that he piloted a small plane and had recently passed a medical. But still there was no sign of him. The members of the Skye Mountain Rescue Team gathered and went out up the hill, staying in communication with the police officer who remained with me and the wife. She was so brave, so composed, and, when I made her some scrambled eggs later on, feeling that she must eat something, she ate them even though she didn't really want them. We drank an awful lot of tea but she declined anything stronger. Somehow the girls got fed during that evening, which felt endless. At two in the morning, there was still no news – vast amounts of sandwiches had been made in the hotel kitchen for the members of the Mountain Rescue Team, who then called off their search till first light, when they planned to call in a helicopter. The wife assured me that she would be all right in her room by herself. I did offer to stay with her, either downstairs by the fire or sitting in her room, but have to admit to being thankful when she said that she would be fine alone because, by then, I felt very much like going to bed myself. Needless to say, Godfrey and I couldn't sleep, wondering how she was and, more importantly, where her doctor husband was.

When we heard the helicopter, we were up and dressed in a flash. For about an hour, it flew low over the hill and then, to our joy, it returned and landed, having found the doctor and his golden retriever. His only explanation was that some sort of magnet had made him go on walking around the hill, even when the track came to an end, and that eventually he and the dog lay down and hugged each other. Although it was only September, it was cold and wet and the dog's thick coat must have prevented a certain measure of exposure. The relief of his wife and of the other guests too, who of course had been aware of what was happening, united everyone in the house. But the mystery of the magnetism – his only explanation for why he had kept on walking – remains with me to this day. The following decade we had a repeat experience but with a different ending.

Pre-Millennium Events

We were approached by the Secretary of the Royal Yacht Squadron who wondered whether we would be able to give a dinner for their Millennium celebration. When we enthusiastically said we'd love to, he came to Kinloch to see the lie of the land and discuss the evening in detail.

This was to be our first really big event and I was determined it would go without a hitch. In front of the South Lodge there was a narrow border of grass which then dropped down about ten feet. We built this out to enable us to put a marquee directly in front of our kitchen-cum-living room, with access through it, down some steps. It was planned for an evening in June 1999 and many of the Squadron stayed with us, as well as in other hotels and lots more on yachts. The evening also included members of the Royal Flying Squadron.

The weather in Skye can never be depended on – it can bucket with rain, freeze or blow to near hurricane strength in June as easily as in any other month. The only thing one could be sure of was the midges, a major consideration in those days and the curse of Highland summers. (Since then we have acquired two midge magnet machines, which have successfully dented the breeding stock to the extent where they really are no longer a problem around Kinloch.)

The guests were to drink champagne in our great room before going in to dinner, to sit at round tables of ten. I hired the furniture from the marquee supplier from North Berwick and the china and cutlery from a supplier in Edinburgh. We planned the dinner carefully and I don't remember any dietary require-ments amongst the 150 guests, which was remarkable for so many people. Dinner consisted of a cold first course of smoked salmon and shellfish. For the main course, we were serving roast venison fillet with one of our best sauces to accompany it, involving a reduction of port and stock with ginger and green peppercorns. I remember summer vegetables and locally grown new potatoes but the other vegetables escape my recollection. For pudding, we had a trio to offer – lemon curd meringue roulade, Scottish strawberries marinated in elderflower and a lemon tart.

Minty and Gavin came over to help with what, to me, was a

mammoth occasion and were invaluable, as were Alasdair and Jenny Alldridge. It is vital on these occasions that the main course is hot and served elegantly but with speed, which is perfectly possible if the plates are heated and there is an efficient line of serving staff. My dread, whether being a guest at a large sit-down function or, worse, when running it myself, is poor service: of half a table having their food whilst the other half are left without until those first served have plates of cold food by the time they pick up their knives and forks. The main course was put out, one table at a time and at record speed. Huge sighs of relief followed as we cleared the detritus before serving out the puddings. Coffee followed with our fudge, for which Kinloch has always been famed, the recipe being from Katherine Robertson.

We did pretty flower arrangements for each table, with two large ones in opposite corners of the marquee, and the windows looked out over the beautiful view in front. It was a chilly evening but dry – lucky us –and the chill kept the wretched midges at bay, so we were doubly lucky. It was with such relief that I woke up the next day with everything safely over. All that was left to do was the sorting out of the cutlery and china into their boxes ready for the kind marquee people who were transporting them back to Edinburgh with the marquee to save us a trip.

Also at the end of that June in 1999 came the other great pre-Millennium event – the European Beef Cattle Show at Chatsworth in Derbyshire. Only one breed was to be allowed to feature in any of the show's cooking demonstrations, and the Highland Cattle Association were given this great opportunity. I was honoured when they invited me to be the demonstration cook. Somehow there was a muddle with the issuing of my invitation and I was only asked to do it some six weeks beforehand. It was an occasion not to be refused, despite the short notice, particularly when I'd had a previous connection with the Highland Cattle Association at the Festival of Food and Farming in Hyde Park in 1989. I have a great respect for the five main breeds of Scottish beef – Highland, Aberdeen Angus, Longhorn,

Shorthorn and Galloway. These are widely acknowledged to be the best in the world due, I am sure, to their slow maturing – they aren't deemed fit for eating until about three years old.

Off I went by train from Inverness via Edinburgh to Derby, where I was met. I had all my prepared foods and dishes for the recipes for the two demonstrations with me, packed into two large chill boxes. I had never before been to Derbyshire and was completely bowled over by the beauty of the countryside and, when we reached the vast park with Chatsworth House at its centre, I determined then and there to return with Godfrey, with more time for a better look.

I was staying at the Cavendish Hotel and my kind hosts drove me around the park, showing me the layout of the show and then we walked through the numerous breeds of cattle, already *in situ* and seeming completely at home. This was my first sight of the Belgian Blue breed. I was aghast that such animals can be bred, with such vast double buttocks that they have to be artificially inseminated, because they can't bear their own weight on their hind legs – ghastly. Can their meat really taste good? I have never had the opportunity to try it and find out, but I was fascinated by them as well as by all the other breeds on show. Not a vegetarian's dream scene but it was an amazing gathering of such a range of breeds, from many European countries as well as from all over the United Kingdom. No one visualised, then, the devastating outbreak of foot-and-mouth disease which lay a mere eighteen months over the horizon.

The following morning, after the inevitable sleepless night worrying about the dems and what I would say and would anyone be interested, I was collected with all my paraphernalia and off we went to the tent at one side of the main show, where a kitchen had been set up ready for me. I put out the trays bearing all the items for each dem. It goes without saying that each recipe involved beef – Highland, of course. I remember that the first passed off all right, as did the second, a few hours later, with the inevitable rush to get everything washed up and back in place in time, which means trying not to appear hurried and therefore rude when, as always happens, people want to talk.

Then it was back into the car, off to the station and on to a Virgin train north which, by the time it arrived at Derby, had no sandwiches or drinks left on board. Luckily, I had been given a picnic and I remember feeling a combination of guilt and relief at the same time as I tried to eat my picnic surreptitiously, trying to ignore the envious stares of others in my carriage who hadn't been able to find food. I comforted myself as they left the train at stops long before my own.

The Millennium

Sometime in 1997, we read in the papers about a castle in Ireland which had been let for the Millennium week for an exorbitant sum as an exclusive one-off. We thought, 'Let's try and do the same with Kinloch – let the whole of the hotel to one party, with us looking after them.' We contacted an agent, who was very hopeful. Huge sums were discussed, most tantalisingly, but the agent thought that insurance might be a problem. It all seemed so far ahead that we put it to the back of our minds.

In 1998, Godfrey and I went to Boston for the AGM of Clan Donald USA and Minty Dallmeyer came to stay at Kinloch to hold the fort in our absence. While we were away, she had a keen enquiry for three rooms for the Millennium. On our return, we discussed things and took the decision to abandon any hope of an exclusive let and instead just accept reservations from individuals. The three of us planned a four-night Millennium New Year bonanza for our guests, arriving on 29 December and departing on 2nd January. We thought about what sort of a holiday we would like if we went to stay at somewhere like Kinloch for such a momentous occasion and we were determined to plan something sumptuous.

We drove the length of England to spend four days at the

Mary Howard Christmas Fair in Hullavington. Our van contained the contents of our shop at Kinloch, my books and all the indispensible kitchen implements I use for my demonstrations. We sat in a row in the van, Godfrey at the wheel, me in the middle and Minty on the outside, notebooks and biros to the fore, writing down exactly what we were planning for our Millennium New Year guests.

This is what we planned and this is how it worked out. On arrival on 29 December, the guests found a printed programme of the events for the next few days, with the assurance that nothing was compulsory and no one need join in if they didn't feel like it. We held a champagne party before dinner in our big living room so that those guests who wished to could meet each other. We handed around canapés, thankful to have Minty and Gavin working with us – four hosts could be far more attentive than just two. Then off they all went for dinner and we had our supper before getting to work on the picnic planned for the following day. A December picnic in Scotland may not sound everyone's idea of fun but, over the previous years, we had picnicked frequently during the winter. Winter picnics mean no midges and often the weather is beautiful, if chilly, and lighting a bonfire makes for great camaraderie. I bought several large thermos flasks and filled them with good soup and we'd baked puff-pastry rolls filled with a mixture of fried onion, apple and pork sausage meat and there were filled baps, rich fruit cake and Stilton and Brie and a chocolate-brownie type of cake. There was plenty of ginger wine and whisky for making whisky macs and red and white wines. We led our guests to the beach on the other side of the Sleat peninsula, Gavin and Godfrey having gone ahead to light the bonfire, and it was great fun. The sun shone and the backdrop of the snow-covered Cuillins set the scene.

Having got home and dealt with the post-picnic clutter, we cleared our big room, set out the drinks and had supper on our knees by the fire. The band then arrived for the reel practice we had planned for after the guests had finished dinner and this turned out to be a great success, with the guests keen to participate. We had a caller who helped with the dances and the evening ended around 12.30 a.m.

The following day, we set off for another picnic, this time with goulash for the main part, accompanied by filled baps again, a different cake, but still rich fruit cake with Stilton and Brie – people's appetites for outdoor food are extremely satisfying. This time we went to Armadale, with a walk around the grounds of the castle after lunch, then home to get ready for the great evening ahead.

We had planned that, after a very special dinner, the guests would come to our great living room where we would dance and sit by the fire there or in the next-door drawing room and then, at midnight, we had a spectacular fireworks display, arranged by Gavin, with a special champagne cocktail to bring in not only the New Year but the next Millennium. It all seemed to work splendidly and we enjoyed it because our guests seemed so happy. The evening eventually broke up sometime the following morning.

A lengthy and luscious brunch was served throughout the first morning of the new Millennium, followed by a hearty walk, led by Godfrey, me and Minty, up the entire forestry track behind Kinloch. When everyone got home again, collapsing beside various fires was the order of the day. Tea was put out on a large table in one of the drawing rooms on each day for people to help themselves to when they felt like it and, that evening, there was another great dinner, followed by cosy chat beside the fires.

Everyone departed during the course of the following morning and, to our glee, many booked for the following New Year and so began the tradition of the Kinloch New Year, pruned slightly from the Millennium, with guests coming for three nights, without the picnics or the giant trek on New Year's Day. We are open for Christmas too, now, with special things planned but at a rather more peaceful pace.

Family Weddings

On 11 November 1999, Isabella married Tom Eveling, from Edinburgh, in the Catholic church in Dornie. The ceremony was followed by a dinner and dancing reception at Kinloch.

The engagement of a daughter is a cause for family celebration, tinged with the inevitable uncertainty when someone else joins the family. In our case, we loved Tom despite our very different backgrounds. His family lived in Edinburgh and his parents were both academics, his father being the renowned poet and playwright Stanley Eveling, who had been Professor of Philosophy at Edinburgh University. We lived in the depths of the country at the south end of Skye and made our income from tourism. Tom, who had read Classics at Bristol University and then worked as a sports reporter for Sky News, had no experience of our sort of lifestyle, nor Isabella of his, coming as he did from a clever family where debate, ranging over a wide number of subjects, was constant. Our family, too, are good at debate but more along the lines of what we should eat at our next meal and that sort of thing – almost always food-related.

The wedding was planned meticulously. We got a marquee from a splendid firm in Berwick-upon-Tweed and I found Jan MacRae, from near Kyle, who undertook the catering for the wedding dinner. We did the first course, the pudding and, of course, the cake, which looked awful, bearing a close resemblance to the hat once worn by Cilla Black at the wedding of a couple from her then TV show *Blind Date*. Isabella had chosen a chocolate cake, which I covered in ganache and, despite its unfortunate shape, it tasted good. My great concern regarding the dinner was that the main course should be served quickly. We had roast fillet of beef with delicious vegetables and gravy and béarnaise sauce and Jan did brilliantly – 240 guests were efficiently served in exactly nineteen minutes.

The service was to be at four o'clock in the afternoon and, during the two days before, we arranged all the flowers, including

163

those on the tables for dinner in the marquee once it had been erected. As any other hands-on mother of the bride will know, when everything is done and the show is on the road, you are knackered. The day before the wedding, when we were having the rehearsal in the church and Hugo's great school and Cambridge friend, the actor Eddie Redmayne, was rehearsing the two anthems that he sang beautifully during the signing of the register, I can remember howling because his voice was so exquisite. I was discovered weeping on the church steps and was kindly mopped up by John and Carol Steele, John having offered his services as chauffeur to the bride in his splendid old Bentley.

The day was indescribably happy but a bit of a blur in my memory apart from two or three things which stand out. One was realising that the small bridesmaids' posies had been left behind in a bucket and never made it to the church and the other was Meriel, in her red satin bridesmaid dress, elegantly trimmed with silvery grey, tucking up her long skirts and vaulting over a pew to give someone a message – typical of Meriel.

The run-up had been hectic because Godfrey and I had only returned from Rio de Janeiro two weeks before. At least two years previously, if not longer, we had agreed to be the guests at the St Andrew Society of Rio's annual Ball and Highland Games, and you do not renege on such an invitation. We were there for two weeks. It was action packed and included a demonstration in extremely hot, humid weather at the very smart hotel where we were staying. We enjoyed being there, apart from my mind constantly straying to wedding arrangements. I longed to know about invitation acceptances. My mother had gloomily predicted that no one in their right mind would want to go to a wedding in Skye in November but she hadn't reckoned on Tom and Isabella's friends. We had only eleven refusals.

Soon afterwards, I had to go to Eggleston Hall, near Barnard Castle on Teeside, for two days of cooking demonstrations. I have been doing dems there for about twenty-five years and am fond of the Grays who live there and run it. Autumn that year didn't seem to contain enough weeks for all that had to be done and, after that, Godfrey, Minty and I departed for York and our first-ever Mary Howard Christmas Fair. It was fun but we had the second of our New Year spectaculars looming, which we were determined wasn't to be merely a pale echo of the Millennium one.

On top of this, Alexandra was to be married that February. She had been nursing on the orthopaedic trauma ward at the Royal Infirmary in Edinburgh, where she had done her training, and she met Philipp zu Guttenberg when he was studying Forestry at Edinburgh University, where he got a First – I am allowed to boast about my sons-in-law. Their romance had proceeded slowly. She had had a disastrous marriage almost a decade before, ending in a painful divorce after three years, so she was understandably wary of any future commitment, as were we.

Her future mother-in-law, Christiane ('Dani'), came to stay at Kinloch with her husband Adolf von Ribbentrop, Philipp's stepfather. We liked them at once. Roland Shaw was also staying and he provided a perfect 'bridge', discovering that they had many mutual friends. Philipp had proposed to Alexandra on the Island of Arran and we gave an engagement party at the New Club in Edinburgh, for which Enoch, Philipp's father, and his wife, Ljubka, came over from Bavaria. His mother and stepfather came too and, thankfully, we all got on like a house on fire and have never looked back.

The wedding had to be a civil ceremony because, although Alexandra was divorced, her marriage was not then annulled. (This takes time, in their case three years, after which she and Philipp were married in the tiny chapel of their house in Austria.)

The wedding, on 24 February, was quite small, as Philipp's father, Enoch, planned to give them a party in April in Bavaria. We were about seventy-five people, with all Philipp's extensive family – his mother being one of nine and his father having three sisters – and his three splendid grandparents travelling to Kinloch from their various homes in Bavaria, Austria and Croatia. We organised a bus to meet their plane, on which I put flasks of hot chocolate, Drambuie and shortbread to sustain them during their journey. Enoch and Ljubka, and Karl-Theodor, Philipp's elder brother, and his wife Stephanie arrived two days before the wedding, as did Dani and Adolf. On the evening everyone arrived, we had a buffet seafood supper in a small marquee. Jan MacRae was, once again, at the helm, and she cooked a marvellous array of fish and shellfish dishes. This was planned because most of our mainland European guests live a great distance from the coast and I wanted them to eat food which Philipp had told me they all love – fish and shellfish – which I imagined was difficult for them to procure fresh.

My parents were staying and several family friends too. My sister Liv and I did the flowers in our small church in Broadford, dedicated to St Maelrhuba, for the family service which was held by Philipp's Uncle Handsel, a priest, following the civil ceremony. Saturday began with an extensive brunch for everyone except the immediate families, who were to accompany Alexandra and Philipp to the home of the registrar, Janet Donaldson, for the civil ceremony. This was performed with great dignity and was very moving. We twelve family members then returned to Kinloch for the brunch and to join everyone else. Early that morning, I had rearranged the flowers from the night before so that everything would look slightly different. Then, after we got home from the splendid family service, tea was served and the marquee had been arranged and tables set for the formal dinner that evening. I did flowers, yet again, for the dining tables – those within the houses and the marquee were mostly blue and yellow, the Guttenberg colours. Speeches were made between each course, accompanied by both tears and laughter, and then the tables were pushed back and we danced.

The following morning, Handsel said Mass in the drawing room of Whippets' Haven, which rather took us short because the drawing room in the old Lodge had been prepared. This was followed by breakfast and then everyone went for walks or just sat around and talked, before going out for lunch in Breakish, nearby, for more seafood. Dinner that evening was in the Kinloch dining room. This may have been a small wedding but it did go on quite a while and by Monday, when everyone left, we all felt that we had had time to get to know one another. Godfrey and I felt that our lives had become considerably less narrow and insular thanks to our new in-law relations who add a welcome dimension to our lives. One can never have enough family, providing everyone gets on, as we most certainly do.

Foot-and-Mouth Disease and 9/11

Philipp and Alexandra's wedding weekend was, for us, the last really good happening of the year 2001. A week or so earlier, rumours of an outbreak of foot-and-mouth disease were rife in Northumberland but we had been so immersed in family and the wedding that it was not until the following week that we realised the rumour had become fact. Godfrey and I went away for two nights, having been given the most luxurious of presents consisting of a couple of nights' stay at Inverlochy. We went to walk along the shore of Loch Morar only to find it out of bounds, due to foot-and-mouth.

Thereafter, it could accurately be classed as an *annus horribilis* not only for farmers but for hundreds of other families and their businesses, throughout the United Kingdom and, later that year, of course, for Americans. Within a very short time of the disease first striking, the whole country was brought to a standstill. Initially, we in Skye thought it wouldn't affect us because we were 200 miles from the nearest outbreak and, watching the news on television, our hearts bled for the numerous farmers who were forced to slaughter their beasts. Whole farms were left silent with empty fields stretching as far as the eye could see. Vast funeral pyres of burning animals could be seen and no transportation of live cattle or sheep was permitted at all.

It wasn't long, however, before we in the tourist industry were also hit with cancellations on a daily basis and virtually no bookings coming in. The Dunvegan estates announced that no walkers or climbers would be allowed on their land and the Forestry Commission followed them, cordoning off swathes of walks, including up the hill behind Kinloch. Motorists driving to Skye from the south have to drive through the Borders, which were so badly hit by foot-and-mouth that no one wanted to go anywhere near them. So we and everyone else in the Highlands were more or less cut off from visitors, which proved devastating for tourism and, to show in some small measure just how hard hit and desperate we all were, the Inland Revenue and Customs and Excise relaxed their stringent collection policy and all tourist businesses were given extra time to pay any monies due, which lasted for about a year.

What made everything so much worse was how appallingly the outbreak was handled, with the official farming and rural bodies seeming hopeless in their actions or lack of them. It was completely natural that the farming fraternity should be in the forefront of everyone's minds but no one seemed to realise just how badly we in the tourist industry had been hit, responsible, as we are, for so much employment. I remember wanting to interrupt when, during Mass one Sunday in Broadford, the priest prayed for the crofters who might be affected during the epidemic. 'What about all the rest of us who are also affected?' was what I wanted to have the courage to shout – 'We in the tourist trade with all its periphery businesses – shops, tour operators, entertainers . . .'

The dreadful outbreak gradually tailed off but the aftermath lingered. Bookings began to pick up as the summer wore on and we were to be full, with an exclusive let to several American families celebrating an anniversary arriving on 14 September that year, for three nights. They had stayed with us before and it was with great delight that we received their reservation and planned their visit, wanting to make it as special as we possibly could.

Godfrey and I had gone to Edinburgh to collect my father from the train, to bring him back to Kinloch for a few days' holiday with us. As we approached the Forth Road Bridge on our way home, our third daughter Meriel rang us on the mobile to tell us that planes had struck the two buildings in New York. She didn't know any more than that. We turned on the radio and listened, aghast, all the way back to Kinloch, as the horrors of that day unfolded.

When we arrived home, we settled my very old father with a cup of tea in front of the television and we raced over to the old Lodge to see how our guests were affected. The day and night that followed took on a surreal quality. Among the several Americans staying, one couple had a son who was a pilot with American Airlines. It was an American Airlines plane which was hijacked in one of the attacks but it was impossible to telephone to find out if, by some awful chance, their son had been a pilot on that flight. We kept the fires stoked up all night, plying our guests with whisky, on the house – the very least we could do – and encouraged those who having gone upstairs to bed but found they couldn't sleep, or needed company, to come downstairs in their nightclothes and find comfort at our fireside.

Once again, everything was paralysed. After a day or two, communication with America was restored but it was several more days before there were flights in either direction. This lost us our three-night block booking for the American families on their long-planned celebration as they couldn't get to us and nor could several Americans who were booked to come to us following the Ryder Cup. It sounds crass to talk finance after such an unthinkable tragedy involving so much loss of so many beloved members of so very many families but we really thought our survival was against all the odds.

A Fishy Business

During this decade, I was approached by a friend of a friend who was starting a business cooking and blast-freezing top-quality fish dishes. He wanted me to be involved and he wanted to use my recipes for the dishes he proposed making and selling. I agreed and, on several occasions, flew down to London to meet up with him and discuss the project. He had also taken on Marcello Tully, a chef with the highest possible credentials. Marcello left his job to take up this new position, having worked for the previous seven years for Albert and Michel Roux – the Roux brothers – who have done so much to raise the standard of cooking in Britain. Marcello had latterly run their sous vide business so he was expertly able for the new fish business. He and I hit it off immediately and he impressed me by his ease of style and his extremely hard-working attitude, as well as his ability to manage, encourage and work alongside his small team in the new kitchen on the industrial estate, which was the base for the fish business. He never once made me feel inferior, as had happened on occasion when I had been in the company of other chefs. I am a domestic cook, too frequently referred to as a chef, which I most emphatically am not. There is a world of difference between what I am and the role of a chef. It's a bit like the difference between an amateur, however good, and a professional, in whatever line of work.

Marcello and I worked together on my trips to the Hertford-shire Industrial Estate, as he made up dishes from my recipes and then blast-froze them. We would then thaw, cook and sample them. I have always enjoyed tasting sessions which could grandly be called research and these were an excuse to eat delicious morsels, cooked by Marcello. Silver vans were purchased by the man whose business this was, with my signature on their sides, and the frozen fish dishes were whizzed around the country, including London. We were dependent on the sales force, some of whom I met during my visits, and I suspect that they were partly responsible for the failure of the business. Also, I think that possibly the enterprise was ahead of its time. The execution of the recipes couldn't have been bettered but we were under-capitalised and, when more capital was sought and obtained from Norwegian ship owners, unfortunately the owner of the business saw fit to increase his own salary and to backdate the increase. The most vital thing to come out of the whole experience as far as we were concerned was that it brought Marcello Tully into our lives – another example of 'cast your bread upon the water and it comes back sardine sandwiches'. More about this in the next chapters . . .

The Shop at Kinloch

Within the old Lodge there was an inner courtyard which had few redeeming features apart from its space. For some years, we had amassed various items which I used in my kitchen and which we sold when away at demonstrations in aid of charities, as opposed to those which were for businesses, for which I was paid. There were also my books, which we sold to our guests, but we weren't organised and had no real premises for a shop. We approached a local joiner, a real craftsman, to ask him to roof over this small courtyard space and turn it into a shop with shelves and, at the same time, we made it into our reception room. It is just off the corridor on the way to the dining room, so is centrally located.

The roof/ceiling was to be Perspex to let in daylight. We assumed that its construction would be a matter of weeks, but we reckoned without our craftsman joiner. About eighteen months later, we were still stacking my books in the bar beside the old till and telephone and, by then, we were extremely impatient to be into the shop and able to arrange all the wonderful kitchen items on the shelves. In the end, it took almost two years – the time it would take to build several houses – but it did look good when we were, eventually, installed.

We had a range of cookware, including Berndes pots and pans, which I use to this day and maintain are the best of all. Above all, they are light, unlike Le Creuset casseroles which, even when empty, are so heavy for someone of my advancing years that it could well be regarded as a health hazard. Our Berndes pans are extremely light, truly non-stick, easy to look after and wonderful to use and I have cooked in them for about twenty-five years. Then there is the potato peeler I love dearly because it just feels right and is sharp and used for a vast number of tasks as well as potato peeling, the vegetable dicers, some beautiful painted and heat-resistant trays and, of course, my books. All the equipment we sell in our shop I use myself, with one exception – the sheets of baking plastic, which many people like but which I cannot use because the feel of them sets my teeth on edge.

The shop is now an integral part of our business and we also sell our ever-expanding range of jams and sauces, as well as our fudge. The problem is that now we need larger premises for the shop and this is built in to the plans for a gentle expansion within the old Lodge. We also have our shop online. Active throughout the year, it is full-time work in the weeks before Christmas. The packing and posting goes on relentlessly and every order is still a thrill!

Recipes
from Our Third Decade

Jerusalem Artichoke Timbales with Hollandaise Sauce

Serves 8

For the Jerusalem artichokes:

900 g (2 lb) Jerusalem artichokes
1200 ml (2 pints) chicken stock
4 large egg yolks and 2 egg whites
salt
freshly ground black pepper
freshly grated nutmeg
200 ml (⅓ pint double cream, whipped

Peel the artichokes – this will leave you with about 675 g (1½ lb) – and cook them in the chicken stock until tender. Drain off the chicken stock and use it for soup later. Put the artichokes into a food processor or blender. Process or blend the artichokes to a smooth purée, then add the egg yolks, one by one.

Turn the purée into a bowl, season with salt, pepper and nutmeg and fold in the whipped cream. Whisk the egg whites and fold them into the purée with a metal spoon.

Divide the mixture between eight buttered ramekins. Stand the ramekins in a roasting tin and pour boiling water into the tin around them. Bake in a moderate oven, 350°F, 180°C or gas mark 4, for about 25 minutes, until the mixture is firm to the touch. Take them out of the oven and leave to stand for 5–10 minutes.

Turn the timbales out of the ramekins on to serving plates.

For the hollandaise sauce:

_____

285 g (10 oz) butter
5 large egg yolks
4 tbsp lemon juice
1 slice onion
salt
freshly ground black pepper
a few parsley stalks, crushed

_____

Simmer the lemon juice very gently in a pan with the slice of onion and the crushed parsley stalks (the crushing releases their flavour).

Make the sauce by melting butter in a saucepan and heating it well. Put the yolks into a processor and whiz, then while still whizzing, gradually add the very hot butter in a steady stream. When it is all added and you have a smooth sauce, whiz in the strained lemon juice. Taste, add salt and pepper to your liking, then pour this sauce over the timbales.

Jerusalem artichokes have one of the most delicious tastes I know. They also have two drawbacks. One is that they are undeniably a fiddle to prepare – they are so knobbly there really is no quick way to peel them (personally I don't begrudge a moment spent in the peeling because they are so good to eat). Their other drawback comes after they are eaten. They are one of the most wind-provoking of all vegetables – even more so than cabbage, onions or beans – and that is really quite something! But they are well worth a little discomfort afterwards. These timbales are very easy to make and are a really good first course for a dinner party.

Marinated Salmon and Smoked Salmon in Lime with Crème Fraîche, Pink Peppercorns and Cucumber

Serves 6

---

450 g (1 lb) organically farmed or wild salmon, skin and bone removed and sliced into neat dice, about thumbnail size
rind and juice of 4 limes or 2 lemons, well washed to remove preservative and dried before grating
½ cucumber, peeled, halved lengthways and deseeded
450 g (1 lb) best quality smoked salmon, diced to thumbnail size
450 ml (¾ pint) crème fraîche
2 tsp pink peppercorns, drained of their brine
1 tbsp torn dill
black pepper

Put the diced fresh salmon into a wide dish and the lime or lemon rinds and juice. Mix thoroughly, cover the dish with cling film and leave it in the fridge for 3–4 hours minimum or overnight. Try to mix the diced salmon around in the marinade once or twice during the hours it sits. The fish will become opaque in colour – it literally cooks in the acid lime or lemon juice.

Cut the deseeded cucumber into neat, fine dice and put these into a mixing bowl. Add the diced smoked salmon, crème fraîche, pink peppercorns and torn dill. When the fresh salmon has marinated for several hours, drain off the lime or lemon juice and mix the fish into the contents of the bowl. Season with black pepper and serve heaped on a white dish and accompanied by warm bread or Melba toast.

Walnut and Parmesan Tart with Caramelised Onions

Serves 6 as a first course or 4 as a main course

For the pastry:

120 g (4 oz) plain flour
75 g (3 oz) walnuts
1 tsp icing sugar
20 or so grinds black pepper
50 g (2 oz) Parmesan cheese, grated
75 g (3 oz) butter, hard from the fridge and cut into bits

Put all the ingredients into a food processor and whiz to the consistency of fairly fine crumbs. Press these firmly over the base and up the sides of a flan dish measuring 20 cm (9 in) in diameter and put the dish into the fridge for at least 1 hour. Then bake in a moderate heat, 350°F, 180°C or gas mark 4, for 20–25 minutes. The sides will slip down but don't worry – with a metal spoon scrape them back into position and bake for a further 2–3 minutes. Cool the baked pastry before adding the filling.

For the filling:

3 tbsp olive oil
50 g (2 oz) butter
2 tsp Demerara sugar
1 tsp salt
20 or so grinds black pepper
6 medium–large onions
2 tbsp medium sherry
2 large eggs and 2 yolks
300 ml (½ pint) single cream

In a wide sauté pan heat the olive oil and butter together and then stir in the Demerara sugar, salt and pepper.

Skin, halve and very thinly slice the onions – this looks a lot but, as they slowly cook, they reduce greatly in amount – and add them to the seasoned oil–butter mix in the sauté pan. Over a moderately high heat and stirring from time to time, cook the onions for about 15 minutes then reduce the heat a bit and cook for a further 25–30 minutes, stirring occasionally to make sure of even cooking. The onions will collapse in quantity and become caramelised. Allow the onions to cool. This stage can be done a couple of days before making the tart as the caramelised onions will keep very well in the fridge.

Beat the eggs, egg yolks and cream together until well mixed.

Spoon the cooled caramelised onions over the base of the cooled walnut and Parmesan pastry and pour the cream and egg mixture in, forking it carefully through the caramelised onions. Bake in the same moderate heat as for baking the pastry, for about 20 minutes or until the filling is just set in the centre of the tart – the last part to set.

Serve warm with a mixed leaf salad dressed with a Dijon mustard vinaigrette.

The flavours of the walnuts, Parmesan and caramelised onions in this tart are supremely complementary.

Lambs' Kidneys with Port and Grain Mustard Sauce

Serves 6

For the sauce:

———

2 medium-sized onions, skinned and finely diced
300 ml (½ pint) stock
150 ml (¼ pint) port
3 tsp grainy mustard
300 ml (½ pint) double cream
½ tsp salt
20 or so grinds black pepper

———

Start by making the sauce – it can be gently reheated.

Put the diced onions into a saucepan with the stock and port and, over moderate heat, bring the liquid to simmering point. Simmer gently, with the pan uncovered, for about 20 minutes. Then stir in the grainy mustard and the cream, salt and pepper. Stirring, let the sauce bubble – the double cream will thicken the longer it bubbles.

For the kidneys:

———

18 lambs' kidneys (I allow 3 kidneys per person)
2 tbsp olive oil

———

Halve each kidney and cut out the core. I find sharp scissors the easiest for this – it takes only a couple of minutes to core the 18 kidneys. To cook the kidneys, heat the olive oil in a large sauté pan and, when it is very hot indeed, fry half the amount of cored kidney halves. As they cook, they curl up. Lift them from the pan onto a warm dish and cook the remainder. The cooking time should be fast – beware of overcooking the kidneys, as this renders them tough.

Mix the cooked kidneys and the sauce together before serving.

I like to serve this with boiled basmati rice and a green vegetable, such as purple sprouting broccoli, or stir-fried Savoy cabbage.

Pheasant Breasts with Orange and Chestnuts

Serves 6

————

6 pheasant breasts
1 tbsp plain flour mixed with salt and ground black pepper
2 tbsp sunflower oil
2 onions, skinned and chopped
300 ml (½ pint) red wine, or stock if you prefer
about 12 chestnuts, shelled and chopped
2 oranges, peel cut off with a serrated knife and flesh chopped
salt and freshly ground black pepper

————

Coat the pheasant breasts in the seasoned flour.

Heat the oil in a casserole dish and brown the pheasant breast/s on each side. Remove them to a warm dish. Add the chopped onion to the casserole and cook for a few minutes till the onion is soft. Stir in the red wine or stock, the chopped chestnuts and the chopped orange. Replace the pheasant breasts in the casserole. Cover with a lid and bake in a moderate oven, 350°F, 180°C or gas mark 4, for 30 minutes.

Take out of the oven, season with salt and pepper and eat as soon as you can.

This is a real treat if you are eating alone. From about December onwards, it is possible to buy pheasant breasts in butchers' shops and most supermarkets. They do shrink as they cook so, if they look small, buy two. This recipe combines the pheasant with the complementary flavours of orange and chestnuts. To save opening a tin of whole chestnuts and freezing what you don't use, buy fresh chestnuts and boil them for 10 minutes. They should then be ready to have their skins nicked and cut off. They taste so much nicer than tinned ones! Alternatively, use vacuum-packed chestnuts. Avoid dried ones like the plague – they have the taste and texture of cardboard.

Serve this casserole with mashed potatoes and with finely sliced cabbage stir-fried with grainy mustard.

Osso Buco with Basmati Rice Gremolata

Serves 6

For the osso buco:

───

3–4 tbsp olive oil
6 slices beef shin, each about 2 cm (1 in) thick
2 onions, skinned, halved and diced
2 sticks celery, peeled with a potato peeler to remove the stringy bits, then sliced quite thinly
2 x 400 g (15 oz) tins chopped tomatoes
½ tsp caster sugar
1 tsp salt
25 or so grinds black pepper

───

In a wide sauté pan, heat the olive oil and brown each piece of shin on either side. As they brown, remove them to a warm plate.

Lower the heat under the sauté pan a bit and fry the diced onions and sliced celery for 5–7 minutes, stirring occasionally, until the onions are completely transparent and soft. Then add the contents of the tins of tomatoes and season with sugar, salt and pepper. Stir as this mixture comes to simmering point. Then return the slices of browned beef shin to the pan with the tomatoes, onions and celery, cover the pan with its lid, remove the handle and cook in a moderate heat, 350°F, 180°C or gas mark 4, for 1 hour. This can be cooked a day in advance but reheat it on the hob until the sauce is gently bubbling and let it simmer very gently, with the lid on, for 10–15 minutes before serving with the rice.

For the gremolata rice:

375 g (12 oz) basmati rice
4 tbsp olive oil
1 fat clove of garlic, skinned and diced very finely
finely grated rind 1 lemon – wash it very well and dry it before grating to remove
    the preservative
2 tbsp parsley, finely chopped

Boil the rice in plenty of salted water for 7 minutes. Pour the pan of rice into a large sieve and then run hot water through the cooked rice. Drain well and tip the rice into a warmed serving bowl. Add the olive oil, diced garlic, lemon rind and finely chopped parsley to the rice and mix thoroughly.

Traditionally, osso buco is made using slices of veal shin but we cannot get veal in Skye and I have substituted slices of beef shin with great success. No one else seems to eat beef shin, but it is extremely inexpensive, has a wonderful flavour and it contains a delicious nugget of marrow in the centre of each slice. The rice accompaniment is, for me, an essential part of the whole delectable taste combinations within osso buco, as it has gremolata stirred through, imparting its lemon, garlic and parsley flavours.

Rich Chocolate, Raisin and Rum Ice Cream

Serves 6–8

———

84 g (3 oz) raisins
6 tbsp white or dark rum
225 g (8 oz) dark chocolate
6 tbsp water
84 g (3 oz) caster sugar
4 large egg yolks
285 ml (½ pint) double cream

———

This basic chocolate ice-cream recipe is the best I know but I
can't claim credit for it because it is the invention of Katie
Stewart, who very kindly let me include it in my book *Sweet
Things*. I have to say that the raisins and the booze were my
idea.

Soak the raisins in the rum for as long as possible –
overnight is best – in a bowl covered with cling film. When you
take off the cling film, the fumes will knock you out for a
second or two!

Break the chocolate into a blender or food processor. Put
the water and sugar into a saucepan. Over a gentle heat,
dissolve the sugar, then boil fast for 3 minutes. Pour the hot
sugar syrup onto the chocolate, cover the lid of the blender or
processor with a tea towel and whiz for several seconds.

When the mixture is quite smooth, add the yolks, one by
one, and whiz until they are smoothly incorporated. Leave the
chocolate mixture to cool.

Meanwhile, whip the cream until it just holds its shape,
whipping in any un-soaked-up rum from the raisins. Fold the
raisins into the cream-and-raisins mixture and the cooled
chocolate mixture.

Pour into a polythene container, cover and freeze.

Take the ice cream out about 30 minutes before serving
and leave it at room temperature.

Brown Sugar Meringues with
Lemon Curd and Whipped Cream

Serves 6

For the meringues:

———

75 g (3 oz) granulated sugar
75 g (3 oz) Demerara sugar
3 large egg whites
a pinch of salt

———

Line a large baking tray with a sheet of baking parchment.
Mix the two lots of sugar together.

Whisk up the egg whites with the pinch of salt till stiff,
then gradually whisk in the combined sugars, a spoonful at a
time, until all the sugars are incorporated.

Either pipe the mixture in even-sized small meringues on
the baking parchment or distribute the meringue evenly, using
2 dessertspoons and bake at a low temperature, 200°F, 180°C
or gas mark ½, for 2 hours. Cool for 10 minutes then lift the
meringues off the parchment and leave to cool completely on a
wire rack. When cold, store the meringues in an airtight
container.

For the lemon curd:

———

110 g (4 oz) butter, diced
110 g (4 oz) caster or granulated sugar
2 large egg yolks and 1 large egg, beaten together
rind of 3 lemons, finely grated
juice of 2 lemons
300 ml (½ pint) double cream, whipped, for mixing with the lemon curd

———

Put all the lemon curd ingredients – but not the whipped
cream at this stage – in a Pyrex dish and set it over a saucepan

of simmering water. Stir until the butter melts and the sugar dissolves. Continue to stir from time to time as the curd thickens. When it is very thick, take the bowl off the heat and leave it to cool.

Fold the whipped cream into the lemon curd, spread a generous amount of this mixture onto one meringue and pop another meringue on top.

Bread and Butter Pudding with Nutmeg and Cream

Serves 6

---

12 slices of malt loaf – the sort with peel and raisins in it, preferably
420 ml (¾ pint) single cream
1 whole egg plus 2 large egg yolks
50 g (2 oz) caster sugar
a good grating of nutmeg
grated rind of ½ lemon
grated rind of ½ orange
1 rounded tbsp Demerara sugar
50 g (2 oz) soft butter

Butter each slice of malt loaf and cut the slices in half.

Butter an ovenproof dish and arrange the bits of buttered malt loaf in the dish.

In a bowl, beat the cream, egg, egg yolks, caster sugar, nutmeg and lemon and orange rinds together, pour this over the buttered malt loaf and sprinkle the surface with Demerara sugar as evenly as possible.

Bake in a moderate oven, 350F, 180C or gas mark 4, for about 20 minutes or until the nutmeg custard is just set.

Serve warm.

Part Four

Our Fourth Decade
2003–2012

Me, a Granny?

This, our fourth decade, has seen much activity. For the family, there was the arrival of grandchildren, the marriage of our third daughter, Meriel, and, in 2010, our move to live at Bellevue, near Beauly. For Kinloch, this decade also saw great change – the most important and exciting being that Isabella and Tom came to live and work with us. And, after eight years of us all working together, we gradually passed responsibility for the whole enterprise to them. Marcello Tully joined us to run the kitchen with his team and we were awarded our Michelin star – the first in Skye – and we were also awarded our coveted red grape Michelin award for our superb wine list. Then, horrifically, in 2008, we very nearly lost the whole business . . .

When Isabella and Tom suggested that they might come to live and work with us at Kinloch, we were amazed. Secretly we had always hoped that one of our 'children' would join us and eventually take over running the business, but somehow the hope had never materialised and we had never expressed our feelings out loud. We were therefore overjoyed by their hesitant suggestion and immediately responded in the affirmative. Isabella had grown up in the hotel environment. Each of our children had known that, however much their help was valued, whatever they did, be it turning down beds or setting a tea tray, it must be done perfectly. They all grew up with a strong work ethic and Isabella, a great organiser, had worked hard in her job, as PA to the head of communications at British Airways. Tom, having worked as a sports reporter for Sky, knew about demanding and varying hours but he had never worked in the service industry. He is an extremely nice man and has a natural rapport with people, but his transition wasn't exactly smooth. Some of the members of our staff, to our great surprise, took exception to Tom and Isabella's arrival and some, it is only fair to say, made things as unpleasant for them as they possibly could. I think they saw the newcomers as a threat to their extremely comfortable working lives.

It is necessary, when writing a book like this, to look back at the bad times, as well as the good, painful as it can be, but, when human nature falls short, it can be cruel and destructive. This unfortunate element in our staff demonstrated that they couldn't care less for Kinloch and the business and, in time, one by one, they departed, a few in a most unpleasant fashion.

There are no two ways about it, Tom and Isabella's arrival and their subsequent roles in our family business have been the saving of it. They know exactly what is required and expected with regard to service, furnishings, bathroom arrangements and everything else. Had our business continued as it was, it would certainly have atrophied. Many of the best food-related businesses throughout Scotland, farming as well as hotels, are family concerns, with some going into second and third generations – Graham's Dairy and MacSween, the haggis makers, to give two examples – but I think that all would agree that having an eye to the future is crucial for survival. Godfrey and I wholeheartedly support Tom and Isabella in their numerous improvements and their awareness of the route down which Kinloch must proceed to succeed. They train all the members of staff joining the team very thoroughly, which is essential, as service must now be the sharpest – there is no room for anything slack or substandard.

When they came to join us, they set up home in the part of the old house which we had built on when we moved there from Ostaig. With our removal to the South Lodge, or Whippets' Haven, this had been empty apart from when it was occasionally let as a holiday cottage. It was ready and waiting for them and it was marvellous having them there.

Within a year, our first grandchild, Billy, was born, followed a couple of years later by his brother, Luke. Before Billy's birth I had viewed the prospect of impending granny-hood with some dismay. Me, a granny? It seemed as if I was to become old overnight and I didn't relish the prospect at all – until, that is, I saw Billy after his difficult birth. He was very ill and had to be put in an incubator with all kinds of tubes attached to him, but I was completely smitten. To hell with thinking that being a granny was a part of being old – nothing mattered except that this precious small being should live and flourish. Thankfully, he did and he was such a beautiful baby – listen to me, soppy grannies don't come soppier! He is now nine, quiet and thoughtful and utterly sweet. Luke too was a beautiful baby, completely different to blond Billy, being dark-haired. He is a vital child and, aged seven, keen to learn and absorb everything. Fortunately the brothers are tremendous friends.

Isabella runs and organises much of my working life. She is the first stop whenever I am asked to do a demonstration somewhere or give a talk or perform whatever role I am called upon to do. She does the arranging and organising in conjunction with me. Having this cushion, as it were, is not only a godsend but much more businesslike than my life used to be. In fact, looking back, I really don't know how we lived our lives without them and it is good to be able to pay them the tribute they so richly deserve, here in these pages.

Food Transition

When we started Kinloch and I was in charge in the kitchen, the type of food I aimed to provide for our guests was, as I have already mentioned, what I thought of as dinner-party cooking. Gradually, however, from reading articles and eating in other establishments, I came to realise that this was becoming passé and that a change was called for. I was able to accomplish this to a certain degree, with the accessibility of ingredients that had formerly been difficult if not impossible to source, but this was not enough to keep up with the times. During this decade, Glyn Musker, a chef who had had the most exacting training, came to work with us. He was a diffident man but very nice and, most importantly, an extremely good, hard-working cook. Before he joined us, he had had a very bad motorbike accident and he found living alone, especially during the winter months, depressing so, after two years, he gave in his notice but, in his typically considerate way, he said he was flexible about when he would leave and would carry on until we found the right person to replace him.

It was at this point that Godfrey and I decided we must aim for a Michelin star. We knew this ambitious goal could take many years to achieve and we knew we must aim for the very best to take over from Glyn. We interviewed a chef who had gained a coveted star in a previous employment and we liked him but he decided against coming to live and work in Skye. Then I had a brainwave. I rang Marcello Tully, with whom we had kept in touch over the years, to see if he knew of anyone who might be up for the challenge. It was a Saturday. He asked all the relevant questions and we talked for ages. He said he would get back to me within two or three days because he knew of a few people he thought might be interested.

The very next morning he rang back and asked whether Godfrey and I would consider him and his wife Claire for the role. Would we! In truth, it had never occurred to me for so much as a fleeting second that he would be interested. He was then working in London, Monday to Friday, in a nine-to-five job where he was responsible for recipe development for a few selected Waitrose stores. Although he was in charge of forty people, he told me he was ambitious and his present job could take him no further. He had met Claire at catering college and she had also been employed by the Roux brothers. They flew up to Skye to see Kinloch and the house we would rent for them and get an impression, however fleeting, of what life would be like. They inspected the primary school in Broadford, for their two boys, Max and Alex, and finally flew back to London, promising to let us know of their decision within days. True to their word, our mobile phone rang as we drove to collect the Dallmeyers with whom we were driving to the south of France for the wedding of the son of friends of ours. Marcello said they would love to accept but that they wouldn't be able to start for six weeks. We were thrilled and the lengthy journey suddenly seemed much shorter. The reason they weren't able to start for six weeks was because they had booked a holiday in Brazil, where Marcello's mother lives. His grandfather had gone there from Edinburgh to open the first branch of an international firm of chartered accountants, many decades before, so he has a combination of Scottish and Brazilian blood, although this was to be the first time he lived in Scotland himself.

Max and Alex are terrific boys and soon settled in to school in Broadford. Once Marcello joined us, the responsibility for the kitchen and its working team was lifted from my shoulders and, to begin with, I couldn't believe it. Our kitchen was antiquated but we had promised him that it would be completely brought up to date and we would take his advice about what would be required. The following winter it was transformed into a fully equipped kitchen, fit for professional chefs to produce the top standard of cooking as conceived by Marcello.

He still maintains that never in his working life has he worked with such top-quality food as he does at Kinloch – that's Scottish produce for you. We are indeed fortunate to have him and he and I agree on most aspects of food and where it comes from. He adheres to my insistence on having it in season – agreeing with me about foreign asparagus all the year round, for instance, and only using game in season. He is a real professional. An inspired chef, he is a peaceful man but he imposes an iron discipline within his domain. There is none of the Gordon Ramsay-style language flying round his kitchen, thank goodness, for to work under verbal assault must be boring and stressful. Nor would there be with any Roux-trained chef who is able to show several years of working with them on his CV – these are the chefs who really count. The Roux brothers' desire to pass on their great knowledge and skills means that they consider it vital to teach, and for their disciples to be qualified to pass on their knowledge to others. The young chefs who work with Marcello are intensely keen from the start or he wouldn't invite them to join his team and the myriad skills they then learn from him are not only good for us at Kinloch but also for the whole of Scotland. Claire (his Claire as opposed to me) is quietly efficient and creates delicious canapés, as well as being responsible for the endless bookwork involved in keeping up to date with all the requirements of health and safety – almost a full-time job.

Marcello had only been working with us for two years when, one mid-January morning, Isabella rang up. Her voice was almost a whisper and I thought something dreadful must have happened. What she actually said was 'We've been given a star by Michelin.' I had to get her to repeat it – I couldn't take it in. We were all in a state of shock, utterly humbled and incredulous that we had achieved what we had striven for so passionately, and far sooner than we ever imagined. The *Michelin Guide* had been published earlier than usual that year – something to do with Amazon – and we were also awarded the coveted Red Grape Award for the first time – something we've continued to do every year since. Once we had recovered from the shock of hearing about the Michelin star, we all went quite mad and celebrated with a carryout curry dinner from the excellent Taste of India, near Kyleakin.

Winning this accolade means more than any other award for two reasons. Firstly, the Michelin inspectors are anonymous and they inspect several times during the year with the guide being published in early October. Secondly, they aren't just looking for the quality of the food but also for consistency. What many people don't realise is that Michelin stars are awarded each year. This ensures that winners can't be complacent and, should we ever lose ours, we would certainly work our collective socks off to regain it. We are immensely proud of every person working with us, and Marcello – an inspiration for everyone – is the first person to give full credit to his team.

Stuttgart and the International Food Festival

The summer before our Michelin star, I received an invitation to represent Great Britain at an International Food Fair in Stuttgart. This invitation assumed that I would be doing the cooking but I told the organisers that, although I would be there, Marcello, with one of his assistants, would be cooking and would also be responsible for the menu planning for the two main events. This was accepted and we got to work and it turned out to be quite an undertaking. The more we discovered about the whole event, the more daunting I found it, and I was thankful for calm Marcello with his organisational skills.

Each of the eleven chefs with their small entourages was staying in Michelin-starred establishments in the region of Baden-Württemberg. Stuttgart is the main city but the region is extensive and our hotel, the Dollenberg, was two hours' drive away, with three of the other chefs staying even further out. The others were from France, Italy, Austria, Denmark, South Africa, the United States, China, Australia, New Zealand and Germany itself. We were each given a driver with a Mercedes to take us wherever and whenever we wanted and ours, Frank, soon became a friend.

Marcello flew out with his assistant, Andy Maclugash, while Godfrey and I drove to Hull and took the ferry to Zeebrugge. The car was packed with all the shellfish and fish packed in dry ice and all the knives and other bits and pieces too bulky or unable to be flown out. In my ignorance, I had no idea we would be staying in the heart of the Black Forest, so we were bowled over by the scenery we drove through to reach the Dollenberg, a large hotel on the side of a hill. The weather was clear and bitterly cold.

We were warmly welcomed by the two generations of the family who own and run the Dollenberg, including the head chef Martin, who was married to the daughter of the owner. Godfrey, Marcello, Andy and I had dinner in the restaurant and went to bed early in order to get up at five the following morning, when we were collected by Frank and driven into Stuttgart for the launch of the festival in the Mercedes-Benz showroom. Marcello, who loves cars, was swivel-eyed as we were led upstairs, passing floor after floor of magnificent cars. There followed an elegant reception with each of the chefs giving a short talk describing their work, how they interpreted food and where they came from. I gave our talk and we were each interviewed by various members of the press.

This wasn't a competition and I looked on it as an opportunity to display Scotland and its food in a showcase. It was a fascinating event as well as one of extreme fatigue. Due to our distance from Stuttgart, our days began horribly early and usually ended early the following morning, so our hours in bed were few – particularly for me, as I need to wash and blow-dry my hair daily in an effort to look smart, or at least tidy.

One of the bonuses of that event was the arrival of Alexandra at the end of our first day. She had driven from Radmer, in the Steiermark, Austria, where she and Philipp and their two boys, Joe and Felix, were living. She had volunteered to come and translate if or when necessary and we had jumped at her offer. After her long drive, she didn't come with us that evening. On our return from Stuttgart we had quickly changed for dinner and our kind hosts drove with us to Baden-Baden, where the Dollenberg family owned the once great casino, with its complex of small shops, notably the chocolatier. Here, I discovered chocolate that surpassed any I had ever tasted – I still dream about their dark chocolate and raspberry truffles, a large box of which I bought for my father's birthday. (He and my mother subsequently had quite a serious row about her eating too many of them.) We are chocolate addicts and, as I consider myself quite a connoisseur, my eulogies about that shop must indicate their quality.

We then drove out of Baden-Baden, up and up a hill with the driving rain becoming snow the higher we climbed. Eventually, at the top, we were met by a wonderful brass band, the men all dressed in Loden coats and hats, playing on, regardless of the snow, which fell on us too because drinks were served outside. We then went into the restaurant, where the heat almost overwhelmed us. We were served course after course, accompanied by schnapps and wines, all delicious, but I began to wonder when the evening would ever end. My main fear wasn't because of our early start the following or, to be accurate, that morning by the time we got away, but for Marcello, who's driver, Martin, went like a bat out of hell, regardless of weather and the twisty roads. Frank, following him, was alarmed by the speed and I was worried for Marcello. When we left the hilltop restaurant, staggering with tiredness, Martin sped away in front of us and was soon lost in the thick mist and driving snow. Frank had a SATNAV system so we had no worries about finding our way back to the Dollenberg, and I almost cried with relief to discover that Marcello had arrived safely by the time we got back.

The following day, we awoke to find some six feet of snow had fallen and this was when Alexandra noticed that Godfrey and I hadn't got winter tyres. Unbeknownst to us, insurance cover is negated if you have an accident in Austria or Germany during the winter without winter tyres. She arranged for the local garage to fit snow tyres for us – costing a hideous 900 euros – which we were grateful for on our way home, when the weather worsened all the way to Zeebrugge.

On the second evening, each chef cooked in the great Stuttgart town hall for the invited celebrities of the city. It was a glittering evening and Marcello and Andy did us proud. By this time, the members of our international group were becoming friends and no one could get their tongues around Andy's surname –Macluglash – so they referred to and called him 'Scotland'. On the last day, Sunday, we were all taken to a vast hall near the airport, bigger than any building I had ever seen – it could have housed the entire Highland Show. Cooking stations were set up and each chef cooked his chosen three courses, which were tasted and commented on by three food judges for a television show. I stress again, this wasn't a competition, no marks were awarded, just comments made, which was much more interesting. Marcello, to reflect the top-quality foods in Scotland, made as his first course a mousse made from hot-smoked salmon from Salar in South Uist, with toasted sesame seeds, encased in smoked salmon from the Hebridean Smokehouse in North Uist. A subtle and delicious taste combination, it was surrounded with a dressing made with dill from the north end of Skye and roasted pistachio nuts. His main course was slow braised pork cheeks with seared scallops and a small scallop soufflé, with a caramelised slice of apple. The combination of pork, in its various forms, with fish or shellfish is age old and this variation of the classic version proved extremely popular. We had tasted and re-tasted it in the preceding week during its creation at Kinloch and I felt really excited about it. For the pudding, we went for a twist on the millionaire's shortbread theme, with a rich dark-chocolate mousse on a thin, crisp vanilla shortbread, with salt caramel – utterly delicious. I had greatly enjoyed doing the research – i.e. the tasting! – during the perfecting of this idea.

At the end of that day, we went back to the Dollenberg, said a fond farewell to Frank, whose company we had enjoyed so much, who was leaving early the next morning to drive Marcello and Andy to the airport, and then the five of us, including Alexandra, had a happy dinner together. In the morning, we said goodbye to her as she drove back to Austria and we, thankful for our winter tyres, headed to Zeebrugge, getting completely lost in Strasbourg on the way. We were saved by a friendly postman who guided us from the industrial estate where the bossy and useless satnav had taken us, abandoned us and then become mute – I nearly threw it out of the window – and led us back on to the main road we should never have left. We felt that we had given Scotland a good representation on the international culinary stage and drove home feeling it had been a job well done.

Scotland and Tourism

This chapter could almost be a book in itself. When we first started at Kinloch, tourism was managed by the Scottish Tourist Board. Any organisation which is funded through taxation, should earn its keep and know its stuff, which sadly doesn't always happen. The Scottish Tourist Board, now called VisitScotland, is publicly funded and there have been many good people working within it. Over the years, alas, there have also been some complete duds with no idea how businesses within the tourist industry are run or what hard work is necessary to keep them afloat. Good taste is often deficient. To give an example, Bob and Jane Taylor used to run their home, Ardsheal House, in Argyll, as a hotel. They earned great renown for its comfort, beauty and delicious food but they were penalised in their rating one year when inspected by a woman from the Scottish Tourist Board because they hadn't put paper doilies between her breakfast glass of orange juice and the plate. The facts that the glass was crystal, the plate Royal Doulton and the orange juice freshly squeezed passed her by. I well remember attending one meeting to discuss quality food and drink, when the Tourist Board official taking the meeting warned us all that it was highly probable that all butter and jams would only be permitted if portion-wrapped – for hygiene's sake. Thankfully, this didn't happen but so nonsensical is the bureaucracy with which we are governed that it wouldn't have surprised me if it had and what would have made it worse is that this particular official had no intention of fighting such a ludicrous requirement if it had been made a regulation. To my way of thinking, a body such as VisitScotland should guide everyone working within the industry, as well as stand up for them.

At this same meeting, I maintained that we in Scotland should take a leaf out of Ireland's book and sell ourselves as a tourist destination through our food. True, the food in Ireland is excellent, but the food in Scotland is better. This was met by the fear that it could have a detrimental result because you can eat extremely badly in some places in Scotland. My response to this negative attitude was that you can eat badly in any country in the world and, in order to eliminate the bad places, you need to engender pride in and awareness of the unsurpassable quality food throughout Scotland, which should encourage more and more people to raise their standards. VisitScotland, I insisted, must be ruthless, refusing to back those who didn't care and took the easy route by buying in ready cooked foods and that they must support only those who really work for the good of their country.

My other great complaint is still ongoing – that Britain is the only country in Europe to charge VAT at its full rate of 20 per cent for all hotels. France charges just 5.5 per cent, Italy 10 per cent and Austria 8 per cent, to give just three examples. No wonder Britain has a reputation for being an expensive destination for holidays. When Godfrey and I first raised this point many years ago at a Scottish Tourist Board meeting, we were told by the chairman that they couldn't raise this point in case their subsidy was reduced due to them making a contrary suggestion. They didn't want to appear awkward. Incidentally, it was at a lunch given by the then Scottish Tourist Board following this same meeting where I ate my first deep-fried Mars Bar. I thought it a bit odd that a body of people who should have been dedicated to promoting all that is the finest in Scotland should see fit to put such an item on the menu of a meal hosted by them – but I must admit it was so delicious that I had another! I think my overriding feeling towards the Scottish Tourist Board for many years was one of complete frustration – that and a simmering rage that so much money, our money, raised through taxes accumulated from our own hard work, should be so misdirected.

Then Derek Reid, a dynamic Scot married to a lovely New Zealander called Janice, was appointed Chief Executive of the Scottish Tourist Board. Having been part of the management buy-out team who acquired Cadbury Schweppes, he had no financial need to undertake such an appointment. But, since buying a hotel in Perthshire, he had become very involved with tourism in Scotland. Owning the hotel had allowed him to see, at first hand, how ridiculous the limitations of the Tourist Board were. It made him want to stir things up and set tourism on a proper course that would do justice to Scotland. I credit him with starting the painfully slow changes necessary to do that and with introducing an awareness of how to sell our country to tourists. It seemed to me that, until Derek took the job, the position of Chief Executive of the Scottish Tourist Board had been regarded as a ripe plum for many who, while good and well intentioned, had no background in the tourism industry.

I remember a much-respected farmer, who was about to take over as Chief Executive, telling me what a wonderful job it was – you got to travel the world and let people know how lovely Scotland is. I told him that the cost of his travels would be much better spent bringing good journalists from those countries to Scotland, to see for themselves all that was on offer, so they could go home and write about it. I seethed at his lack of understanding about the task he had undertaken and because our money was contributing to the travels of someone who was so woefully ignorant of the tourist industry.

One of the problems was that those responsible for enticing visitors to this country were under the narrow-minded impression that Scotland was somehow unique, and that it would sell itself just by being 'Scotland'. Whenever I was given the chance, I told them that Scotland is one of many countries with staggeringly beautiful lochs, rivers, moors and mountains. Austria, Switzerland, Germany, Norway, Sweden, France, Italy and Spain, all these and many more can give Scotland a run for its money in regard to scenery and history and they all have good and interesting food but I maintain that we have the best, top-quality food in the world due, I'm convinced, to the fact that the Highlands and Islands, and a good chunk of the Grampian region too, are designated the last wilderness area in Europe. Therefore, it stands to reason that the food raised on the land – beef and dairy cattle, lamb, pork, venison and game, not to mention fish – and that grown in the land – vegetables, arable crops and fruits – must benefit from the purity of the land, air and waters, both fresh and salt.

Over the past couple of decades, chefs and cooks throughout Scotland have used this unbeatable local produce to win awards from all round the world and those who teach in the catering colleges have raised the standards amazingly. The food scene in Scotland is an increasingly exciting one, becoming more so every year despite the efforts of cynical journalists, such as A. A. Gill, who write that it is impossible to find good food north of Glasgow and Edinburgh, discrediting themselves in the eyes of those who know better.

Scotland has become home to people from all over the world and they have brought their national dishes with them, adding to the adventure of eating out, if you do a bit of research and go to the right places. But, as with Scottish fare, the quality of the food depends on its ingredients. Whether you eat pasta with ragu or lamb tikka masala or any other of the myriad dishes from another country, the marriage between the recipe and the quality of its ingredients is the secret for its success. This was gradually acknowledged by the Scottish Tourist Board as it morphed into VisitScotland and, at last, food became a valuable marketing tool. Wendy Barrie is one who worked tirelessly in her role as Chief Inspector for Taste of Scotland and she was assiduous in her work. She had the gift of being able to encourage those working within the industry, running hotels or guest houses, and show them with gentle tact how to improve. It was a sad day when she left. Wendy now runs her own flourishing consultancy and I always relish working with her when we find ourselves on the same platform – we are in complete agreement about food in Scotland and a lot more besides.

Another problem is how to convince the politicians that the responsibility for Scottish tourism merits the full-time attention of one Minister, or Secretary, as they are called in our SNP government. Despite knowing the colossal financial contribution the tourist industry makes to government funds and what a vast source of employment it offers, trying to get our industry the attention it deserves has been like pushing water uphill. I'm convinced this is a relic from the time when going into the tourist industry was thought to be a last resort for those who couldn't find another job. You can still detect this misapprehension when tourism is discussed as a career option and it seems to have percolated through to those in government. In all other European countries, working in the tourist industry is deemed dignified – a job to be undertaken as seriously as any in other industries. The hotel schools in Austria and Switzerland produce superb students who are proud of their work and we can do it too, but we have been slow to learn.

Three men have led the way when it comes to quality of service in Scotland – Michael Leonard who, as I've already mentioned, was managing director of Inverlochy Castle for many years, Stewart Spence of the Marcliffe at Pitfoddels, outside Aberdeen, and Peter Croome at Skibo Castle, near Dornoch. These three, in their individual ways, have taught the skills of serving people to many others – skills that, I contend, can't be taught in a four-year degree at university. No lecturer seems to realise the importance of teaching their students the simplest facts, such as the need to smile when taking telephone bookings or enquiries – that a smile can be heard, not just seen. I was horrified, at a meeting chaired by Donald Macdonald of Macdonald Hotels many years ago, when we were told how we should aim at only employing people with degrees in our industry. I spoke up, disagreeing vehemently. I think of Michael Leonard, who always maintained that he far preferred taking on new staff for Inverlochy who had no training or experience because then he could teach them himself. And I think of Tom and Isabella, who invest a great deal of time in the training of new staff for Kinloch because they know how crucial it is to the success of the business.

In our present government at Holyrood, John Swinney holds the post of Cabinet Secretary for Finance, Employment and Sustainable Growth and he is also responsible for tourism. This is certainly an improvement on the last government, when the Secretary for Tourism was also responsible for energy, but I won't be really content until one person has sole responsibility for tourism and nothing else, in order to give this vital industry the full attention it deserves. I do, however, feel extremely positive about VisitScotland these days. Chairman Mike Cantlay is an extremely able, dynamic man for whom nothing is too remote or too minor to be visited. I was impressed when he came to Portree to the opening of the new Youth Hostel, shortly after his appointment. The Chief Executive, Malcolm Roughead, is also a man of action, who has the right feel for tourism these days. Godfrey and I had the opportunity to work closely with four members of the VisitScotland staff during the three days we were in Lyon together – about which more later. As well as having fun with them, we worked together and we were impressed by just how hard-working they were and by the fact that all four of them were fluent French speakers.

I really do think the future of Scottish tourism is improving, though there are still some awful glitches, not least the online central booking system which is currently a disaster, but I feel confident that these problems will be ironed out. VisitScotland needs to gain stature so that people are proud to join it, not keen leave it, but they must feel that their annual subscription is worth it.

I realise I have written this whole chapter on the Scottish Tourist Board/VisitScotland without once writing the word 'hospitality'. This is a glaring omission because hospitality is – or should be, anyway – the bedrock of our tourism industry. Hospitality is a welcoming smile and a concern that the guest, whether having a cup of tea or just asking the way, feels that you mind about them. I get an inner glow when, as often happens, people abroad tell me how hospitable they find the Scottish people. I am not a Scot nor ever will be despite having lived and worked here for forty-two years but I feel pride on behalf of the Scots. We have wonderful scenery and a fascinating history and so do many other countries – but it is the Scots who are known for their hospitality.

Politics

At this point I feel I should add a résumé of our politics. In 2006, when Godfrey told me that he intended to vote for the SNP, I said, 'But what about me? I am English.' I feared I might be ethnically cleansed and sent packing back to where I come from in the north-west of England. Godfrey's reasoning for his support for the SNP was that devolution was something he foresaw would be the disaster it was proving to be, certainly for those of us living in the Highlands, and that the Conservatives hadn't a hope in hell of ever being elected for at least a generation. The Labour MSPs seemed an uninspiring lot, and were kept in power by the LibDems.

Several people who knew Donald Dewar well have told me what a nice, though indecisive, man he was, but, in my opinion, he must have been ill advised. To give the go-ahead for such a monstrous building as the Holyrood Parliament, which went way over budget, smacks to me of vanity. The thought of more years of the same stretched ahead of us and Godfrey wasn't alone in thinking that the SNP should be given a chance to govern, especially given that the party was led by Alex Salmond. I've already mentioned Roland Shaw, who started Premier Oil. He was one of the wisest men I have known and, early in our acquaintance, when he was staying with us, he said to Godfrey and me that, if our path ever crossed that of Alex Salmond, to heed him because he was clever and Roland liked him. Remembering this, I wrote to Alex Salmond and asked him some questions, including whether the SNP would impose a bed tax on visitors to Scotland.

The next thing I knew there was a telephone call from Alex himself, reassuring me about my concerns. Subsequently, we got to know him and like him – and his wife Moira – and, over the years, we saw a lot of them. When the time came, we both voted SNP and several of our acquaintances were scathing in their condemnation of us. Our reply was 'Consider the alternative.' We thought Scotland had been well served during their first term of office. Before the 2011 election, I was asked to do a small party broadcast for them, to support Richard Lochhead, who is the Cabinet Secretary for Rural Affairs and the Environment. Richard is good at his job, works tirelessly and travels throughout Scotland and the Islands. He is responsible for food and drink exports, which topped the £1 billion mark in 2011. I said I'd gladly do the broadcast on two conditions. One was that I would say what I think and that everything must be left in the short programme. Although we support the SNP, like many others who voted for them, we do not want to split from the Union and want Scotland to remain part of the United Kingdom. True to their word, they left in what I said on this important point. And the other thing I asked was that, if they won the election, they should put one person in charge of tourism. As I have said earlier, in their previous administration, the man with responsibility for tourism also had responsibility for energy. I didn't quite achieve what I was asking for but tourism did get an excellent Cabinet Secretary in John Swinney, who is also responsible for finance. These two are closely connected, whereas energy has little to do with tourism.

As is now history, the SNP got in with a thumping majority and we all await the result of the referendum – not its outcome because we are sure the Scots will not vote for separation (we fervently hope not, anyway) but we wait to hear when and how the referendum will be worked and worded. Scotland is an exciting country to live in and several people, including my sister Milla, have remarked how it feels as if it has more pride and confidence in itself. I give the SNP full credit for this.

Cooking Demonstrations in Lyon

One day in 2009, I received an email inviting me to do two days of cooking demonstrations, followed by lunch for the attending journalists, in Lyon, in the middle of France. In my ignorance, I hadn't realised that Lyon is considered the gastronomic heart of France but, nevertheless, I said yes, I would love to take this on, but that I would have to have Godfrey with me, as my other half and vital companion. Minty was unable to accompany me because she now runs a very successful bed-and-breakfast business and the visit to Lyon was due to take place at the end of May, a particularly busy time for Minty. I planned the food for each demonstration and the lunch I would make, trying to use the ingredients I like best, to give a good idea of the quality of the foods to be found in Scotland. VisitScotland were brilliant and they took no shortcuts in sourcing every item I had chosen and shipping it all out to Lyon. I chose smoked salmon from the Hebridean Smokehouse in North Uist and hot-smoked salmon from Salar in South Uist. We had fillet of beef and I made a roasted pineapple and coriander salsa-cum-salad to go with it. The cheeses we brought included a wonderful Brie from Connage Highland Dairy near Ardesier, Isle of Mull cheddar and Humphrey Errington's Dunsyre Blue, from South Lanarkshire. We also took rich fruit cakes and vanilla sponge slices, all baked with no preservatives whatsoever, made by the famous Harry Gow Bakery, whose headquarters are on the industrial estate at Culloden, in Inverness, but who also have shops in and around Inverness – they have happy customers over a wide area. And we took small, rich dark-chocolate cakes made by Marcello from Kinloch. I was determined to show off the fabulous food to be found throughout Scotland.

It helped that easyJet had recently launched a direct Edinburgh–Lyon route. When we arrived and made our way to our hotel, it was with some dismay that we found the lift wasn't working and we had to trudge up three flights of stairs in a fairly dingy hotel. But, after all, none of us was there to be lavishly looked after so it was right and fitting that we should all stay in such a place. It was central and we could walk to the beautiful main square of Lyon, where a bookshop with a restaurant and a kitchen was to be our headquarters for the two days of our stay. Much more important than our personal comfort, however, was the lamentable lack of sufficient cold storage space. The food had all arrived safely, to our relief, and Godfrey and I immediately set about searing the beef fillets and roasting the pineapples, then finding somewhere cold enough to store everything. A young chef, Jerome, who took classes in the restaurant kitchen, then appeared and he proved to be a lifesaver in our predicament, as well as becoming a friend. With his assistance, we got all the food prepared for the demonstrations over the following two days, as well as for the buffet lunches. Jerome recommended the name of a small restaurant for dinner and, when we arrived, their young chef heard that we were all from Scotland and came to talk to us. He told us that his great friend, with whom he had worked for some time, is Tom Kitchin, the renowned chef who famously got his first Michelin star just eight months after he opened his first restaurant, The Kitchin, in Leith, and had just been given a star for his second restaurant, Castle Terrace, in the centre of Edinburgh. Small world.

Our four fellow travellers from VisitScotland were easy companions whose company we enjoyed more with each day that passed. At the first demonstration, when I began by saying that the best food to be found in the world was that from Scotland, there was laughter and some giggles. But, by the end and as they ate lunch, the laughter became less and a serious interest was shown. Almost my best moment was hearing a journalist say, '*Mon dieu*, this Brie never came from Scotland!' and being able to tell him that it most certainly did. That they stayed, on both days, till after four in the afternoon, just eating and eating, was the best possible reward for any of the six of us. Going by my rule that it is better to have excess than not enough, I had vastly overestimated the amount of food we took with us but the stalwart VisitScotland girls got all of the surplus packed and shipped back home. Altogether, we had a fascinating time. Lyon is beautiful, Jerome became a new friend, the whole experience was fantastic – exhausting but exhilarating. Another wonderful opportunity that we had seized and loved.

TripAdvisor

For many hoteliers, TripAdvisor can be a nightmare. A part of Expedia, it is an online reviewing system where users can post their comments about hotels, restaurants, holiday rental properties and visitor attractions. Unlike all professionally published guides, however, TripAdvisor relies entirely on input from the public – at least this is its stated aim. Whilst many people use it responsibly to leave justified and useful comments – and we are immensely grateful to those guests who are kind enough to write genuine reviews about Kinloch – it can also be hideously abused. Because it permits anonymity from its contributors and because it is completely unable to police the reviews, it can license outpourings of bile from people who have never spent a night in, eaten at or visited establishments they write about. Such reviews can come from sacked members of staff or from fellow hoteliers who see others as a threat. They can be written by self-important people who dream up things that are wrong, without any personal experience or proof, and who get some sort of kick out of publishing something deeply damaging on the internet. Sometimes the contributions are written by guests who disliked their visit but were too craven to tell the management of their dissatisfaction when they paid the bill and, under the safe cloak of anonymity, let rip with an outburst usually out of all proportion to their perceived bad experience.

There is another very unattractive aspect of TripAdvisor that we, at Kinloch, have experienced on several occasions over the years – the threat. A guest, on paying the bill and telling us that they enjoyed their stay, asks for a discount for no reason and, when politely refused, then tells us to wait and see what they intend writing on TripAdvisor. In the spirit of never paying a ransom, we have always held our ground and refused.

It is almost impossible to get the completely fabricated reviews removed from the website even when they seem clearly to have been inspired by malice. The acid test, when it is a first review, is that TripAdvisor can be distinctly uncooperative and elusive. Driven by the anger and near desperation of hoteliers throughout the country, some of whose businesses have been damaged by the unfairness of reviews posted on TripAdvisor, the Advertising Standards Agency launched a formal investigation, in September 2011, into their claims that they provide trust-worthy and genuine reviews. As I write, a brave hotelier from Wiltshire is suing TripAdvisor for loss of business due to them claiming that reviews praising her hotel are fake. I cry shame on the bed-and-breakfast establishments, guest houses and hotels who advertise TripAdvisor in their entrance halls. And I also decry those establishments who coerce their departing guests to write a TripAdvisor review for them. In my view anything done to perpetuate this website should be frowned upon. And anyone who does seek to get reviews written about them does so in the knowledge that inevitably, in time, their actions will come back to bite them.

My advice to anyone looking up an establishment on TripAdvisor is to read as many of the reviews, bad and good, as possible and draw your own conclusions, but to remember that TripAdvisor can't be regarded as reliable.

The Family

This was another decade of great change and family happenings – luckily for us, almost all wonderful. Meriel, our third daughter, met Peter Strang Steel again at a party in London, after about twelve years. Their courtship had their four parents holding their breaths because it was the romance of dreams – April Strang Steel is Meriel's godmother and she and Colin have been amongst our dearest friends for many years. When Peter proposed with a jelly sweet ring, up the hill behind Kinloch, tears of joy were shed. Their marriage took place in January 2007, with many dire prognostications about what we would do if the weather was bad. My response was that the weather in Skye can be awful any month of the year and that January is no less predictable than June – there had been devastating gales on two of the Saturdays in the previous June. This didn't prevent us from feeling rather nervous, even though, and Godfrey and I had devised a fallback plan. In the event of strong winds, we would decamp to the Broadford Hall. But we needn't have worried. With permission from the Clan Donald Lands Trust, we erected a large marquee on the gravel in front of Armadale Castle – it would be the first Macdonald family wedding to be held there for almost a century. In the week before the wedding, April and I, with the help of other friends, arranged the flowers, transforming the marquee into a warm, glowing spectacle of pale pink, shocking pink and orange. We also did the flowers in the Church of Scotland church in Broadford which was kindly made available to us by the minister, Ben Johnson, for a number of reasons. Monsignor Robert Macdonald came out of retirement to officiate. We had excellent caterers from Angus and, looking back, I feel happy whenever I remember that day. Peter and Meriel now live in Edinburgh with their small son, Milo, and his smaller sister, Kitty Willow.

This decade also brought us five other grandchildren – Billy and Luke, already mentioned, and Philipp and Alexandra's Joe, Felix and Antonia. Dearly as we love our grandsons, we were secretly hoping for a granddaughter this time and we got Antonia, who bears an almost uncanny resemblance to her mother at the same age. And now we have Kitty Willow as well – two grand-daughters, lucky us.

Hugo, meanwhile, left Cambridge, having gained a First in Arabic and the history of the Middle East, but he wanted to be a journalist. He was an intern for ages, working for a magazine owned by Richard Desmond, called *Happy*, a name that caused my mother to shudder. To Godfrey and me, internships are a method of employing people to slave for you for little or no payment but we were assured that it is the price to be paid for experience, as I am sure it is. Governed as we are by draconian employment laws, it does seem strange, however, that interns can be given such a raw deal.

By a lucky coincidence, on the day that Richard Desmond pulled the plug on *Happy*, Hugo was offered a job on the prestigious *Wallpaper* magazine. This was a wonderful chance and he loved working there but then, when we were in Bavaria for Antonia's christening, he was fizzing with anxiety because he had been approached by *Monocle* to be their new design editor. He explained that *Monocle* was the magazine created by Tyler Brûlé, a Canadian–Estonian who had founded *Wallpaper* and then sold it after about ten years to start *Monocle*, a magazine which is both design and news orientated. Hugo had already had two interviews and was waiting with bated breath to hear whether or not he was actually being offered the job. The internet at Essbaum, Philipp and Alexandra's house, was in the throes of being installed and reception was spasmodic so it was no wonder poor Hugo was like the proverbial cat on a hot tin roof. It was worth the suspense and he was offered the job, which he accepted with alacrity. As I write, he is one of their team, working round the clock on his job as design editor, as well as broadcasting live and recorded interviews for the new Monocle 24 radio station on the internet. Heralded as the new World Service, the station has, so far, been received to huge acclaim. Hugo says how very lucky he is and what a fantastic experience it is to be part of the inception of a radio channel. He travels widely, loves it all and works like a dervish.

One aspect of family life during this decade hasn't been so

happy and positive. My beloved parents both suffered strokes. Pa's, in 1998, was devastating, leaving him unable to swallow for many days and, when he eventually could, it was only with some difficulty and still is. He chokes easily so conversation and eating at the same time is impossible. His speech, too, was affected but he has worked valiantly on this over the years. A stroke is a cruel affliction and, despite the Stroke Association's efforts, its profile is never that of cancer or any other severe illness although it can change life dramatically in a blink. Following this, at the age of eighty-four, Pa could no longer write or hold a golf club. Having been a good and keen player, he had played for the seniors and is the oldest living member of Royal Lytham St Anne's Golf Club. Just before his stroke he had written a book, *A Sailor's Survival*, recounting his experiences in the Royal Navy and also giving an account of his capture, escape and recapture and imprisonment in Colditz. A wonderful, kind man, he has kept his sense of humour, but it has been sorely tested and now, aged ninety-seven, he is so frail it is heartbreaking.

Those of us lucky enough to have had parents worthy of love and respect automatically look up to them but, during this decade and towards the end of the last, we have had a reversal of roles and I, with my sisters Milla and Livy, feel we are now in charge. Initially, when it became apparent that my parents couldn't manage at home, we were somewhat frustrated, on occasion, when, having found someone to come in and help them, my mother had decided he or she wasn't needed and so they left, one after another.

Their first move was into The Gables, a beautiful Abbeyfield home in Kirkby Lonsdale. It had been set up by my mother about thirty-five years before, with the proceeds of a generous anonymous bequest, left to provide a house which was to be divided into flats for the elderly. The residents could have lunch and supper cooked for them, to be eaten communally in the dining room, but they would make their own breakfasts in their rooms. My parents had a bedroom, bathroom and sitting room, which we all decorated, and we tried to make the move as easy as possible for them. Having to give up your home is a terrible blow, especially when you have lived life to the full, and everyone shared their misery. We three sisters, helped by our loyal, supportive husbands, tried to make the day of the move as painless as we could. We made their beds and turned them down, lit the fire and left *The Times* on a large kelim-covered stool beside it. But, of course, this devastating change in their lives meant that their independence was at an end. Things went gradually downhill thereafter.

There followed a broken pelvis for my poor mum, followed by a heart attack, which meant that she needed to be looked after beyond the capability of the staff at The Gables. Brant Howe, just up the road, was more of a nursing home so she was transferred there and my father was able to walk up the hill to visit her twice a day. But then came the decision to move my mother again, this time to Hartland House, in Milnthorpe, an extra-care home run by Abbeyfield where there was a larger room available. This caused dramas because my father had, by this time, stopped driving so how was he to visit my mother, when they were both allergic to the very word 'taxi'? In their eyes, taking a taxi was the very height of extravagance. There followed a month during which, between us, we organised a network of saintly cousins and friends who drove him to Hartland and back and then it was agreed that he should move there too.

Having been such a vital, organised person, my mother hated old age but in a way her final year was strangely peaceful. In early January of that year, she fell and hit her head on the corner of a chest of drawers and was rushed off to the Lancaster Royal Infirmary. We were in Bavaria looking after Alexandra and Philipp's three children while they were in New York and we got the news of my mother's fall the night they got home. We drove straight to the hospital on our return the following day to find her in the dreadful Medical Assessment Unit, where she was kept for two days. We were told that she had broken her skull and then that she hadn't and she was then moved to the geriatric ward. What she suffered, in the ten days she was there and on later occasions when she had to be re-admitted, was beyond any of the horrors people complain about in care and nursing homes and which we had disproved in the three we had experienced. It was as bad as anything one reads in the newspapers from time to time, about the neglect and ill treatment of the elderly and those who are incapable. We couldn't be there twenty-four hours a day but, when we were, we made sure that she had all the sips of water she wanted, we cleaned her teeth and tended her in any way we could. And we complained. On the subsequent occasions when she had to go back to the same ward following small strokes, things had definitely improved. In June, after a final visit to the geriatric ward, she had deteriorated to the extent that she was bed bound. She was very peaceful and not really with us mentally, though, now and again, she would surprise us by coming out with something pertinent and astute.

It is the care and nursing homes that seem to get the bad press but our experience is completely the opposite. We have found nothing but love and consideration for both my parents, often in the face of their frustration at their total dependence on others – a frustration which could be cloaked in abruptness. In my mother's case, losing her eyesight due to macular degeneration was the worst thing. For someone like her who had been an avid reader, retaining, unlike me, total recall of everything she read, it was almost impossible to learn how to feed discs into machines when unable to see buttons or read the contents of the disc.

She died on 10 December 2010, having been bedridden for the final six months. That she was nursed so expertly in a care home rather than a nursing home speaks volumes for Hartland, and she couldn't have been in better hands. When she died, we had been there for many days, seeing her and helping Pa in any way we could. We all felt blessed to be part of such a united family and to have had a mother from whom we had learned so much, formidable and even quite frightening though she could be at times, and she was deeply loved by her entire family. The three of us now visit Pa there as frequently as we possibly can, trying to go at least each month and often more, but it is never enough, and I know I speak for Milla and Livy when I say that we live with guilt when we aren't there.

Our Banking Crisis of 2008

Kinloch, like any other largely seasonal business, makes its money over the really busy months, which are April till the end of October. During the other five months, the cash surplus is gradually depleted and an overdraft facility is required to cover the final few months before we become busy once more. Our bank, the Clydesdale, renewed this facility each year. In 2008, none of us – not Godfrey or me, nor Tom or Isabella – had any premonition that anything would be any different. We had been a profitable business for thirty-six years, with security far in excess of the comparatively small sum needed for our overdraft.

We should have smelt a rat when month succeeded month with no overdraft assurance but we weren't at all suspicious because the then business manager at the branch in Portree kept assuring us that the formalities were just taking a bit longer that year and we had no need whatsoever for concern. So when, on 17 December that year, she (the business manager) informed us in a curt telephone call that our overdraft facility wouldn't be renewed for that coming year because the Clydesdale Bank had a new policy of not lending to any tourist-related business in the Highlands, we were stunned. Our horror was compounded by the fact that we could speak to no one at the Clydesdale – the business manager had left abruptly and we couldn't get anyone in Inverness to talk to us either. We knew we would run out of money fairly early in the New Year, with no overdraft to prop up the business until the spring bookings started to flood in.

We were not alone in our predicament. Up and down the

country, businesses were in the same situation as we found ourselves but no one in the banking sector seemed to care, always hiding behind someone else. We knew that, without a borrowing facility, there was no way that our business could survive financially from January to March and we realised that, without a miracle, there was no alternative to placing the business in administration.

Our miracle came – we were kept going by two generous family members, who lent us sufficient bridging finance and we shall never cease to be grateful to them. Had they not stepped in to help us, Kinloch Lodge would no longer be in our ownership and there would be no Michelin star in Skye. That all our years of hard work came so close to ending makes me give thanks daily for our salvation. I have to state that the Clydesdale Bank, at a local level, behaved reprehensively. They could not have cared less what happened to the business and all those employed by us.

Our faith in the Clydesdale Bank has been restored to some extent since we were taken under the wing of their west of Scotland business manager in Oban. 'Frank the Bank', as he is affectionately known to us, is very interested in the business, keeps in close touch and, for the first time in our lives, I think it is fair to say that we feel our bankers understand the business we are. The fact that he, Frank, comes to visit us speaks volumes. This was a salutary and terrifying episode and made us realise that absolutely nothing in the financial world can be taken for granted these days and also how fortunate we were in having an alternative source of funds available to us when many other small businesses did not.

Employment Law

When employment regulations were first introduced, the aim was to protect employees from unscrupulous employers but, over the last forty years or so, the pendulum has swung in the opposite direction. These days, for small businesses, the legislation is so complicated and easy to fall foul of, however inadvertently, that it is a very real impediment. The employment law in the UK is ridiculously complicated and fraught with expensive legalities and so stacked against the employer that it is ludicrous. Successive governments always say they are going to simplify legislation for small businesses but nothing ever seems to happen.

As I write this, plans are under discussion regarding the employment law but the changes proposed seem too mild by far, though some change is better than none. One point being considered is that someone must work for a business for two years before they can take their employer to an industrial tribunal, but this is being strongly objected to by some liberal Members of Parliament who have clearly never run their own business or been subjected to the hell of being taken to a tribunal with absolutely no justification (which has happened to us twice), apart from it being an easy way for claimants to gain a generous sum of money at the expense of their wretched employer. I fervently wish that every MP was made to run a business before being elected to make employment laws. When employing people, you can't be too careful but, however much care is taken, there is no guarantee that you won't be taken for a ride, sworn at, threatened, stolen from or that your precious business won't be at risk from those in your pay. In almost forty years of running Kinloch, we have had our fair share of the negative sides of being an employer that I often yearned for a business which could be entirely family run – but a family that would include Rachel MacKinnon.

We like to think we are good employers. We really care about those who come to work with us, helping them in any personal crisis, which most families have at some time, and we have had many more employees we have loved and with whom we stay in touch than otherwise – though it is hard to forget the rare exceptions.

Kinloch and Design

Tom and Isabella's arrival to help us at Kinloch, bringing with them a fresh vision for the future, was the salvation of our image. Familiarity with a much-loved house can cause a sort of blindness to its shortcomings and this had happened with us. I could see no further than the need for new curtains and carpets throughout . . . including in bathrooms. Very gently, I was made aware of the need to modernise – carpets in bathrooms had long been replaced by more hygienic slate or tiled floors. I agreed and my only stipulation was that they must have underfloor heating. Isabella was introduced, quite by chance, to John Davidson, an eccentric and charming journalist who also advised on design. He warned us that our relationship with him would not be long-term because that was how his working life ran.

We loved him and he must be given credit for many of the improvements which brought us into the 21st century. It was John, with his unerring eye, who rehung pictures and chose and organised curtains, carpets and bed hangings. He would appear with his car bursting with acquisitions, all perfect for whatever their destination (though not, alas, all budgeted for). Increasingly, we feared for his arrival which, despite our pleas to call a halt, even temporary, to the re-equipping of Kinloch, would herald the need for a cheque on his departure.

He was true to his word. When it came to redesigning the dining room, he suggested a very, very dark pine green, almost black, decor. I had a sleepless night, knowing that this had to be vetoed. The following morning, I told him that I felt this wasn't right for Kinloch – that it would be altogether too gloomy on a rainy morning. He couldn't have been nicer about it but that was the parting of our ways – just as he had warned us in the beginning. We have so much to be grateful to him for.

My father used to say, 'Cast your bread upon the water and it comes back sardine sandwiches.' At one of our demonstration weekends at Kinloch, some years earlier, we had had a guest called Sue Evans, a designer who lived on the Wirral. The sardine sandwiches came about because, while she was staying, she asked if I would consider going to the Wirral to do a demonstration in aid of a local cancer charity and I said I would. Godfrey, Minty and I stayed with her and her husband Gary and she showed us round her business, Castree Design. So, when John left us, we thought of Sue and Castree and asked her to come and see us, which she did. She started on her designing in the dining room, transforming it to perfection. She has the gift of getting the feel of a place and interprets what we want before we realise what that is. Our relationship with her is comfortable and ongoing and we feel completely safe in her designer's hands. Some people find change difficult to accept and two of our guests have hated ours sufficiently to have been tactless enough to tell us so, which has hurt a bit. Luckily, far more of our guests have loved what has been done to both houses, the South and North Lodges.

The Clan

Godfrey severed all connection with the Clan Donald Lands Trust during the last decade, feeling that it had become impossible for such an organisation to be run by trustees from all over the world. Some of these far-flung members think they know how things should be run at Armadale, on the Isle of Skye, but are so disconnected with reality as to be laughable. As I write, the only trustee with real experience of running a Highland estate and all this entails has resigned. He was a very good friend of Godfrey and the fact that he is also a renowned authority on Gaelic literature and everything connected with the Gaelic culture makes his departure an even greater a loss to the CDLT. The other trustees should have fought tooth and nail to keep him on board but no one would listen to him on the matters which really count.

The CDLT was just a small part of Godfrey's commitments. Being High Chief of Clan Donald – the only clan to have a High

Chief – brings responsibilities and continuous contact with members of Clan Donald worldwide and we both feel extremely lucky to have this element in our lives, despite there having been moments when time spent with members of the Clan have clashed with other pressing calls on our time. On one such occasion, I had to stay at Kinloch to help before the wedding of the daughter of one of our friends, which had coincided with the annual tour in June of the Clan Donald Chiefs. This rotates between parts of the once extensive Lordship of the Isles and that particular year was in Northern Ireland. Meriel, our third daughter, accompanied Godfrey in my place.

Usually, we try to join this annual tour for several days and far and away my favourite of its locations is Islay, with Finlaggan the site where the Clan parliament used to sit. In those days, the 1100s or thereabouts, the clan was well organised, incorporating its own chancellor, poet and legal advisers – in fact, representatives from every branch of life, all safely kept within one of the branches of the clan family. Clan Donald was unique in this respect.

We have often attended the annual general meetings of the Clan Donald USA, which vary each year from state to state. We loved our time in Alaska, which was organised by the north-west region of Clan Donald USA but, equally, we enjoyed the opposite end of that vast country, when we attended the meeting in San Antonio, Texas. We visited the Alamo, where the Daughters of the Revolution arranged for a most moving ceremony to be held in the honour of Clan Donald. Over the decades Godfrey has been made an honorary citizen of Georgia, by the then Governor of Georgia, Jimmy Carter, before he became President, and of Texas.

The High Commissioner of Clan Donald USA is appointed every three years and, when his term is up, he is succeeded by his deputy. (So far there has been no female High Commissioner but this will change shortly.) This is an internal USA appointment, rightly so, but Godfrey will have known the candidates over the years.

I try to keep in touch by writing a letter twice a year for the American publication *By Sea by Land*, which reaches Clan Donald members around the globe as well in the States. We have many good friends among the Clan, people we look forward to seeing when they visit us from America, Australia and New Zealand, as well as South Africa, Belgium and Holland and several other countries – Clan Donald truly is worldwide. Godfrey holds his role as High Chief in great regard and also with a measure of humility. It is his through birth and Hugo will succeed him (may that day be many years away) as the 38th High Chief of Clan Donald.

The Claire Macdonald Brand

As I have said, we opened our small shop at Kinloch early in this decade and take some of our stock to sell at charity demonstrations to cover our costs, including our jams, chutneys and savoury sauces. Isabella works tirelessly to further the brand and she has been helped hugely by the Local Enterprise Company (LEC), under the expert chairmanship of Robert Muir, and also by Highlands and Islands Enterprise. The advice and knowledge provided by both these organisations restores flagging faith in government bodies. And, not long ago, we were joined by Fergus Watson, a wizard when it comes to marketing and placing our products, as well as anticipating future product development. Each month since he joined us, he has attracted a growing list of outlets for our range and, equally important, the number of those who reorder is increasing.

The Kinloch Monthly Menu Club was the idea of Tom's friends and, now in its eighth year, it has proved a success. I write an introduction, followed by six seasonally inspired recipes, with hints and tips accompanying them, Tom suggests wines to go with the different dishes and Isabella tidies it all up, writes a shopping list and emails them to our subscribers at the start of each month.

We find that it has become a popular Christmas present and it is flattering how many of our subscribers re-subscribe each year. I enjoy writing it, as well as the response I get from subscribers.

We had a brief flirtation with the idea of opening a shop within a shop in a new development being built in Yorkshire. We were introduced to the developer who'd asked us to do it but, when we got down to details, it transpired that he wanted us to sign up for a five-year lease with too high a rent, and Fergus advised us against committing ourselves to such an unproven venture. It was a wise decision but a shame in a way because we'd have been near where I come from in the Lune Valley. Had it not been at such an early stage of development, we would have given it a try, but it was too risky at the time and with such a lengthy commitment.

Selling at Christmas fairs is another outlet for the contents of our shop, usually with Minty helping us. She and Godfrey are much more expert at selling than I am. I can do the salesman bit but the trouble comes with the money. I can neither add up nor use a calculator – as I've already mentioned, I have a complete mental block when it comes to anything to do with figures. Godfrey and Minty dread seeing me wrapping up an object and being handed a credit card, both of them knowing that there will inevitably be a muddle. I do try, really hard, but without much success. The worst thing I ever did was to use the credit card machine to bash up some delicious chocolate-coated honeycomb, some of the sticky stuff somehow getting jammed in the works. This was not popular, I have to say. But I am able to smile and chat in the face of occasional bad manners, where Godfrey can be quite put out. Selling from behind a stall is a revelation. Some members of the public treat you as if you just weren't there and talk about the things you are selling as if you were invisible. On one occasion, somewhere in Sussex, Godfrey's patience reached its limit. Two women picked things up off the stall and put them back down, not terribly carefully, and they riffled through books, with no respect for the pages. They were, to be blunt, what

Godfrey, Minty and I refer to as MOBs – Mean Old Bitches. When one of them picked up a bar of the superb Isle of Skye soap we sell, looked up and asked him, 'How long does this last?' he replied, 'It depends on how often you wash!'

The Disappearance of a Guest

In our second decade, I wrote about a guest who went missing just before dinner (no connection with the approaching feast, we were later reassured) and I mentioned that we had a second experience of the same thing a couple of decades later on. We had just arrived in Italy for our October holiday in 2009 and we were talking on the telephone to Alexandra in Austria, who asked us whether we had heard from Isabella and whether the disappeared guest had been found. Isabella, bless her heart, hadn't mentioned anything about this, not wanting to disturb our holiday, but, of course, once the cat was out of the bag we rang to discover that the poor things had two dramas on their hands. The first and worst was that one of the guests, who had arrived to stay for a few nights with his sister to celebrate her birthday, hadn't returned from a short walk. This had happened twenty-four hours earlier and, in spite of a thorough search, there was no sign of him. To my horror, I heard that there were sixty men, composed of three mountain rescue teams plus police, using our large kitchen-cum-living room as their base and being fed and looked after as they searched for our guest. (A few weeks later, Isabella received a very kind letter thanking her and telling her that never, on any other search, had they all been so well fed and looked after.)

The guest, who had been widowed two years before, was extremely fit. A keen fell walker who ran marathons, he appeared much younger than his eighty years. His two sons flew up when informed of his disappearance and, as day succeeded day, with no clue as to his whereabouts, they vowed to remain at Kinloch until he was found, which necessitated them having to move from room to room because of bookings. Isabella and Tom became extremely fond of these men and of their aunt. At dinner on her actual birthday, the reason she had come to Kinloch, she remarked to her two nephews that it was rather an awful way to celebrate a milestone birthday, to which one of her nephews said, 'Just you wait till you see what we've got lined up for your next birthday!' This sort of gallows humour greatly endears us to people, however strange that may sound.

During this fraught time, there was also a very strange single man staying. He had a large dog with him and a wooden box. He ate breakfast at Kinloch on the first morning of his five booked nights but he never ate another meal in the dining room. Isabella and Tom were looking after our whippets, Plum and Willa, and this man's dog attacked Plum. Isabella told us that it was just a superficial leg wound and nothing to worry about at all. One morning a few days after this event, we rang for a daily report and to see if there was any news of the missing guest. Tom answered the telephone and told us that Isabella was out fetching Plum from the vet following his operation. He said they would be very careful nursing him and that the drain in his extensive bowel wound would be constantly checked as instructed by our marvellous vet in Broadford, Alan Sime. I said I had understood that he had only had a superficial bite on his leg. 'Oh no,' said Tom, 'it was really bad – his bowel was bitten into and he has had a major operation.' So, on top of everything else, poor Isabella was nursing our elderly dog. We credit her, together with the surgical skills of Alan Sime, with his complete recovery. Isabella told the police about the strange guest and they investigated, to discover that the wooden box contained the ashes of his wife and that he was grieving for her and this was the reason for his constant hugging of the box.

Our poor missing guest wasn't found and all sorts of theories were put forward to explain his complete disappearance. Eventually, his sons had to leave to try to pick up their lives with their own families, their aunt having departed a few days after his disappearance. Gradually the police left and the wonderful members of the mountain rescue teams, who had searched so thoroughly, disbanded after a few days but an individual team continued to search occasionally, as did the police. Eventually, in the following February, three members of the Highland Constabulary, searching one day, discovered the body. One of our dreads had been that he had fallen and broken his leg. He had, in fact, walked much further than anyone had thought possible. As darkness fell, he must have become disorientated and he walked down a deer fence to the shore, found himself unable to get along the shore so walked back up the deer fence and, during this climb, he suffered a heart attack, which was what killed him. His room key was in the pocket of his waterproof jacket. We were all so grateful for his discovery and that, at last, the mystery was explained.

Our Move to Bellevue House on the Black Isle

During the ghastly winter of 2008–09 the seeds were sown for change, and this is how it came about. On 29 December 2008, we had a fire at Kinloch which made a great hole in the roof of the old lodge. It didn't set off any of the numerous alarms, because it was caused by a great spark from the chimney which fell back onto the roof and burnt through into the attic, where there are no alarms because no one thought there would ever be a need for any up there. The fire was only discovered when some guests going over for breakfast early that morning saw flames leaping from the roof. Amazingly, considering the large amount of roof damage, we were lucky enough to lose the use of only one bedroom but that room was due to be occupied the same night and we were completely booked up. The only solution was for Godfrey and me to remove ourselves from our bedroom, spring clean it and use it for the incoming guests.

Had I realised when I woke up that morning that I would need to clear out of our bedroom and bathroom within a few hours, I think I might have considered running away. But, with the help of Wendy Morrison, always a stalwart during the many years she worked with us, our room somehow acquired anonymity and was transformed into a guest bedroom. Godfrey and I took up residence on mattresses on the floor of our large kitchen-cum-living room for several nights. This had benefits – though not many, to be truthful – and drawbacks. The benefits were sleeping with a log fire and watching the flickering on the ceiling, and the dogs loved having us on the same sleeping level as them, so the four of us were very snug. The drawbacks were, first, a complete lack of any privacy whatsoever. All sorts of items from our living room are borrowed for use in the dining room when we are very full, so the staff would forget that we were sleeping there and would come in to get more chairs or plates or cutlery, finding me, on one occasion, standing in my bra and knickers as I was changing for the evening. No one noticed and we didn't really mind, everyone was too busy, but we began to yearn for some peace. It then began to dawn on us that maybe the time had come for us to think of looking for somewhere else to live, where we could have a bit of space.

Our lives had been so immersed in the hotel for so many years that we hadn't noticed how our space had been encroached upon and, in fact, we had never minded at all. But once it began to take root, the idea of having our own house became extremely attractive. The trouble was that all our capital was tied up in Kinloch so we would have to look for somewhere to rent. But where? I am a great believer in fate and, yet again, fate took a hand in the form of Minty. On hearing of our tentative thoughts, she said that she might know of just the house, and she and Gavin led us to Bellevue House, on the Black Isle, between Beauly and Muir of Ord. The house was almost derelict when we first saw it, but we were completely smitten nevertheless. It is owned by a local family and managed by a trust for which Minty is a trustee

– hence her knowledge. The trust had recently sold some land and intended doing up Bellevue with some of the proceeds so, yet again, we were lucky to be involved before any uncomplimentary architectural designs had been irretrievably applied. It is a very special house with a wonderful atmosphere and well-proportioned rooms. For the years that we are to live here, we want to enhance it and, if possible, leave our stamp on it.

Over that year, we had a lot to do with the builders, who were marvellous, and we were allowed a say in what should and should not be done. The factor, Nigel Fraser, of Strutt and Parker, kept a watchful eye and all the negotiations were smooth and easy.

We moved in on 11 December 2009, at the start of a bitter winter. Waking up in our new bedroom on that first morning, with utter peace around us, was so exciting and the excitement hasn't quite worn off yet, and nor has our pleasure in being lucky enough to live here. We are in-comers to the locality but we have lots of good friends living nearby, and we love being surrounded by farmland. We are in the middle of land farmed by two different families, and everyone is patient with us both asking endless questions as to what is being grown, sown, reaped, why, what about the cattle, the sheep . . . They must wonder where we lived before but it is all so different, here on the beautiful Black Isle looking across the Beauly Firth, to living on the equally beautiful west coast of Skye.

Perhaps we wouldn't be so happy had we severed all connections with Skye which, of course, we haven't. Skye will always be home, and we are there once or twice most weeks that we are here – the drive only takes an hour and a half. When we told people that we were moving over here, several voiced their disapproval – one even describing us as rats leaving the sinking ship. Our departure was viewed by some as a failure in our loyalty to Skye and Kinloch and we were thought to be abandoning Isabella and Tom. Few people realise how pressured life can be living in and running a hotel – we didn't, ourselves, until we moved away.

People were judgemental and we heard, as one does, so much rubbish, but time disproves untruths.

As for Tom and Isabella, we had all worked together happily and successfully almost 100 per cent of the time and been mutually supportive throughout. Our partnership has been an extremely good one, and we have had – and still do have – great fun when we do things together. But it is good for them to have some space, too, with us a small distance away. They are now responsible for the running of Kinloch and they do a really good job. It is death to a business to remain stationary and they have a clear vision for the future, including discussions with the planning department for an extension to the kitchen, the dining room, and for four more bedroom suites. Most of the bathrooms are due to be upgraded during the winter of 2012–13. I fear that the desire for glitzy bathrooms has altered people's expectations more than any other aspect of design. Some of our bathrooms are as the architect designed them almost fifteen years ago and, possibly unfairly, I wish he had thought ahead regarding space because, even in those not-so-far-off days, it was almost de rigueur to have both a bath and a shower in each bathroom and we are extremely limited for space, despite the fact that all now have elegant large-tiled floors with underfloor heating.

Innovation in the form of a small spa opened at Kinloch in November 2011. Isabella and Tom had long been mulling over their hopes to create one and this is the beginning. A skilled masseuse has come to live in Tarscavaig, on the other side of the Sleat peninsula, and she will be providing all the treatments on offer, ranging from reflexology to Indian head massage, with a whole body's worth in between.

There is nothing to beat a family-run business and ours is now well and truly into its second generation. Godfrey and I will be going to Kinloch tomorrow, for me to do cooking demonstrations on Saturday and Sunday, so this story ends where it began – with a winter weekend of cooking dems at Kinloch.

Recipes
from Our Fourth Decade

Hot- and Cold-Smoked Salmon and Toasted Sesame Seeds Mousse

Serves 6

———

6 ring moulds, 6 cm (2½ in) in diameter
175 g (6 oz) cold-smoked salmon
100 g (4 oz) hot-smoked salmon, flaked into a bowl
125 ml (3 fl oz) double cream
25 g (1 oz) sesame seeds, toasted
1 tbsp lime juice
1 tbsp lemon juice

———

I tend to make this using only cold-smoked and hot-smoked salmons but Marcello has been known to use his home-cured salmon to line the moulds.

Line each ring mould with cold-smoked salmon.

Put the remainder of the cold-smoked salmon into a food processor and whiz till very smooth. Briefly whiz in the double cream then scrape the contents of the processor into a bowl. Mix in the flaked hot-smoked salmon, the toasted sesame seeds and the lime and lemon juices, which will cause the mixture to turn firm due to the action of the citrus juices on the cream.

Divide evenly between each smoked salmon-lined ring mould and neatly fold the ends of smoked salmon over the top. Press down firmly on each – I use the round top of a small jar. Then carefully lift the ring from each mould, turn each the other way up and put one mousse on each serving plate.

If you like, serve with roasted pistachios scattered around the edge, some salad leaves and a few drops of dill vinaigrette.

I make these up to two days in advance of eating. They are so delicious and so easy.

Spicy Courgette Fritters

Serves 6

For the batter:

175 g (6 oz) self-raising flour
1 tsp salt
15 or so grinds black pepper
1 large egg
300 ml (½ pint) milk

Mix the batter ingredients together into a smooth batter and
leave it to stand.

For the courgettes:

6 medium-sized courgettes
4 tbsp olive oil
1–2 fat cloves of garlic, skinned and finely diced
½ tsp dried chilli flakes
½ tsp salt

Cut both ends off the courgettes, halve them lengthwise and
cut each half into small dice about the size of the nail on your
little finger.

Heat the olive oil in a wide sauté pan and fry the courgettes
over a moderately high heat, with the diced garlic, chilli flakes
and salt, stirring from time to time, for about 12–15 minutes,
until the courgettes are turning golden.

Take them off the heat and allow to cool for 10 minutes.
Then stir the courgettes and garlic into the batter.

Wipe out the sauté pan with kitchen paper, add more olive
oil and cook the courgette batter in spoonfuls, allowing each
fritter about 45–60 seconds' cooking before turning them over,
using a plastic spatula, to cook for the same time on the other

side. The fritters should be golden brown on each side. As they are cooked, lift them onto a warm serving plate covered with a couple of thicknesses of kitchen paper, to absorb oil. Serve them warm.

I like to serve these with a good home-made mayonnaise but they are also good with crème fraîche containing snipped chives.

Seared Scallops with Cauliflower Purée and Crispy Pancetta

Serves 6 as a first course or 4 as a main course

For the scallops and pancetta:

12 king scallops, including the vivid coral crescent which is their roe
3 tbsp olive oil
20 or so grinds black pepper
120 g (4 oz) pancetta

Stab the coral on each scallop with a sharp knife in two or three places – this will prevent them bursting when the scallops are searing. Put the scallops into a wide dish and brush them with olive oil. Grind black pepper over them and leave, loosely covered, in the fridge till 10 minutes before cooking them.

Chop the pancetta into small dice, grill or fry until crisp and drain off the fat.

For the purée:

1 medium–large cauliflower
rind of 1 lemon, finely grated
a good grating of dried chilli
1 level tsp salt
15 or so grinds black pepper
2 tbsp extra virgin olive oil
1 heaped tbsp finely chopped parsley and snipped chives mixed

Trim the leaves off the cauliflower and cut away any tough stalks. Break the cauliflower into florets and steam them until just tender.

Put the cooked cauliflower into a food processor with the lemon rind, grated chilli, salt and pepper and whiz till smooth. Whiz in the 2 tablespoons of olive oil. Scoop the mixture from the processor into a bowl. Stir in the chopped parsley and snipped chives and the crispy pancetta.

Cook the scallops by heating a dry sauté or frying pan until very, very hot. Add the scallops and don't be tempted to move them for 30 seconds – they literally sear in the extreme heat of the pan. Turn them over and cook for a further 25–30 seconds (count!) on the other side. Lift them onto a warm dish – don't stack the cooked scallops because they will then continue to cook in their trapped heat.

To serve, put a spoonful of the cauliflower purée in the middle of each of 6 warmed plates. Put 2 seared scallops on each plate – 1 either side of the spoonful of purée. Serve warm.

Rare Beef Salad with Roasted Pineapple and a Ginger Dressing

Serves 6 as a first course or 4 as a main course

For the beef and the roasted pineapple:

1 pineapple, left whole and with the skin on
675 g (1½ lbs) fillet or topside of beef
15 or so grinds black pepper
1 tsp salt
150 mls (¼ pint) olive oil

This is a special occasion main course dish or, alternatively, it can be a first course and is very good served before a fish main course such as the salmon en croûte.

Roast the pineapple whole (roasting it whole intensifies its flavour) in a hot oven, at 450°F, 220°C or gas mark 7, for 30 minutes, then allow to cool – leave the oven on for the beef. When cold, slice off the skin and cut in half then in quarters. Cut away the tough core. Dice the flesh of the cooled roast pineapple. You want about 5 tablespoons for the dressing – eat any of the remainder.

To roast the beef, coat it all over with grated black pepper and 1 teaspoon of salt and rub in the olive oil. Sear over a high heat in a dry pan, then roast in a hot oven, at the same temperature as for the pineapple, but for only 10 minutes. Allow the beef to cool, slice it thinly and arrange it on a serving plate.

For the ginger dressing:

2 tbsp soy sauce
1 tbsp sesame oil
juice of ½ lime – about 1 tbsp
1 tsp runny honey
a piece root ginger, finely minced – about tsp

1 fat clove of garlic, skinned and very finely chopped or grated
2 tbsp coriander, chopped
1 pinch of dried chillis

―――

To make the dressing, combine the diced roast pineapple flesh with the other ingredients, mixing well, and spoon this down the centre of the sliced beef.

Guinea Fowl Braised with Bacon, Shallots and Savoy Cabbage

Serves 6

3–4 tbsp olive oil
3 guinea fowl
12 banana or large shallots (or 24 small shallots)
6 slices of back bacon
600 ml (1 pint) chicken or vegetable stock
½ tsp salt
15–20 grinds black pepper
2 bay leaves
1 Savoy cabbage
1 tsp white wine vinegar

Heat the olive oil in a large stew pan or casserole big enough to hold the 3 birds. Berndes make one called an oval roaster (we sell them!). Note that, if they are large birds, only two will be needed but the guinea fowl we buy here are only sufficient for two people.

Brown the guinea fowl well all over. Meanwhile, cut the rim of fat from each bacon rasher and slice the bacon rashers into thin strips.

Skin the shallots but leave them whole.

Once the guinea fowl are browned, lift them onto a large warm dish and add the shallots and bacon strips to the pan. Cook until the shallots are browned all over, stirring occasionally. This will take 5–7 minutes. Then add the stock, salt, pepper and bay leaves to the pan and put the browned birds in with these ingredients. Bring the stock to simmering point, cover the pan with its lid and cook in the oven at a moderate heat, 350°F, 180°C or gas mark 4, for about 45–50 minutes.

Take the birds from the casserole, lifting them out carefully and dripping off excess juices. Put them onto a dish and cover loosely with foil to keep them warm.

Removing any dark-green outer leaves of the Savoy cabbage as you think necessary, chop it in half and cut away its tough core. Cut each half into 3 wedges.

Add the white wine vinegar to the vegetables and bacon left in the pan or casserole and then add the wedges of cabbage. Replace the lid and cook on the top of the stove for about 5 minutes or until the cabbage is tender. Try to keep the shape of the cabbage wedges as they cook.

Carve the guinea fowl and put the carved meat back into the pan with everything else. Alternatively, you can serve the carved guinea fowl on warmed plates, spooning the bacon and shallots and a wedge of cabbage beside the carved fowl.

This is very good with beaten mashed potatoes and with roast fennel or with a mixed leaf salad dressed with vinaigrette.

There may well be bits of this left over. It can then be made into soup – strip any meat from the guinea fowl carcasses and add more stock to the pan or Marigold stock powder made up with boiling water.

Roast Rack of Lamb with Minty Hollandaise Sauce

Serves 6

For the rack of lamb:

———

3 racks of lamb, French trimmed
175 g (6 oz) pinhead oatmeal
30 or so grinds black pepper
1 level tsp flaky salt
1 tbsp olive oil

———

Trim excess fat off each rack of lamb.

In a bowl, mix together the pinhead oatmeal, pepper and salt with the olive oil. Put the trimmed racks of lamb in to a roasting tin lined with baking parchment – this just makes washing up so much easier afterwards – and cover each rack with the oatmeal mixture, as evenly as you can.

Roast in a hot oven, 400°F, 200°C or gas mark 6, for 15 minutes. This will give you fairly rare meat. If you – as I do – prefer lamb pink rather than red, then leave it for a bit longer. To serve, either slice each rack in half, or slice into individual chops and arrange on a warm serving plate.

For the minty hollandaise sauce:

———

300 ml (½ pint) white wine vinegar
2 slices onion
1 tsp black peppercorns
2 bay leaves
a few parsley stalks, crushed
½ tsp salt
4 large egg yolks
220 g (8 oz) butter, cut into small bits
2 tbsp mint, finely chopped

———

Put the wine vinegar, onion, black peppercorns, bay leaves, parsley stalks and salt into a small saucepan and simmer till the liquid is reduced by half.

Meanwhile, put a saucepan containing water on to simmer and be sure that you have a Pyrex bowl that fits snugly into the pan. Using a flat whisk, beat the yolks in the Pyrex bowl, put the bowl on top of the pan of simmering water and beat the bits of butter into the yolks, a bit at a time, not adding the next bit until the previous bit has melted. You will get a thick emulsion of yolks and butter in the bowl. When all the butter is incorporated, strain in about 1 tablespoon of the flavoured and reduced wine vinegar and mix it in well – the vinegar must still be hot. Taste and add more if you like a sharper flavour to the sauce. Take the bowl off the pan and pour the thick hollandaise sauce into a thermos flask to keep it warm and to allow you to wash up the saucepan, bowl and flat whisk. Before serving, stir the chopped mint into the sauce – if you add the mint too soon, it turns an unattractive brownish colour. Serve in a warmed bowl.

I love to serve pieces of potato roasted in olive oil with rosemary and whole cloves of garlic with the lamb. Green vegetables, such as cabbage, kale, winter greens or spinach, also go very well.

The small amount of time spent reducing and flavouring the wine vinegar is well worthwhile. Any surplus can be stored in a screw-top jar in the fridge. Reheat before using. Too many people still think that hollandaise sauce in all its variations must be made at the last minute. This is simply not the case at all!

Dark Chocolate Mousse with Salt Caramel

Serves 6

For the salt caramel:

———

120 g (4 oz) granulated sugar
300 ml (½ pint) double cream
1 tsp vanilla extract (if at all possible let this not be Madagascar bourbon vanilla
    because it just doesn't taste of vanilla)
1 tsp Malden salt flakes

———

Start by making the salt caramel because it has to cool before it can be made up with the chocolate mousse.

Put the granulated sugar into a small heavy saucepan over moderate heat. Shake the pan from time to time as the grains of sugar slowly dissolve. Don't try to speed up this process – burnt sugar tastes bitter and acrid!

Heat the cream in a saucepan.

As the granulated sugar dissolves it becomes a molten amber mass. When all the sugar has dissolved, pour in the cream – which *must* be double to allow it to thicken as it boils. The heat of the cream will dissolve the molten sugar into itself but stir as this is happening and then let the caramel boil for 3 minutes. Stir in the vanilla and then allow the caramel to cool. Stir the salt flakes through the cooled caramel.

For the chocolate mousse:

———

25 g (1 oz) butter
175 g (6 oz) dark chocolate
3 large eggs, separated
pinch salt
75 g (3 oz) shelled pistachios, stir-fried for a few minutes, to slightly toast them,
    and then cooled

———

The chocolate mousse couldn't be simpler. Break up the chocolate and put the pieces into a Pyrex bowl sitting over a pan of almost boiling water, making sure the bottom of the bowl doesn't touch the water, and allow the chocolate to melt. Stir the butter into the melted chocolate and then beat in the egg yolks, one by one. The heat of the chocolate will cook the yolks and, as well as getting thicker and thicker, the chocolate mixture will also become glossy.

Put the egg whites into a bowl, add a pinch of salt and whisk to a stiff and glossy mass – adding salt will increase the volume of the whites as you whisk them. With a flat whisk fold the whisked egg white quickly and thoroughly through the chocolate mixture. Leave to stand for 10 minutes.

Measure 1 cm (½ in) of salt caramel into the bottom of six small glasses and then divide the chocolate mousse between the glasses, spooning it over the salt caramel.

Scatter a few toasted pistachios on top of each mousse.

Frangipane Tart with Lemon Pastry and Apples

Serves 6

For the pastry:

———

120g (4 oz) hard butter, straight from the fridge, cut into bits
175g (6 oz) plain flour
1 rounded tbsp icing sugar
rind of 1 lemon, finely grated

———

Make the pastry by putting all the ingredients into a food
processor and whizzing to the texture of fine crumbs. Press
these firmly over the base and up the sides of a flan dish or tin.
Put this into the fridge for at least an hour and then bake
straight from the fridge at a moderate heat, 350°F, 180°C or
gas mark 4, for 20–25 minutes or until the pastry is biscuit
coloured. The sides will slip down but, using a metal spoon,
you can easily scrape them back into place up the sides. Cool
the pastry base.

For the filling:

———

4 good eating apples but, if they're small, you might need 6
175 g (6 oz) flaked or halved almonds
120 g (4 oz) soft butter
120 g (4 oz) caster sugar
1 large egg beaten with 2 large egg yolks
a few drops of almond extract
rind of 1 lemon, grated
50 g (2 oz) butter melted
1 rounded tbsp granulated sugar

———

You can still find British-grown Cox's or use Pink Lady or any
other good-tasting eating apple. I do not include Golden
Delicious in this (or any other) category.

Peel, quarter and core the apples and then cut each quarter into 3 slices.

Pulverise the flaked or halved almonds in a food processor, dry-fry until pale golden in colour and then cool. I do try never to buy ready ground almonds – their flavour isn't a patch on those you grind yourself.

Beat together the butter and sugar until soft and pale and then beat in the cooled dry-fried pulverised almonds, the beaten egg and yolks, the almond extract and the grated lemon rind.

Spread this mixture over the cooled baked pastry base. Arrange the apples on top, pushing them down into the almond mixture. Brush the surface with the melted butter and sprinkle the tablespoon of granulated sugar evenly over the surface.

Bake in the oven at a moderate heat, 350°F, 180°C or gas mark 4, for 25–30 minutes or until the apple slices are turning colour. Take out of the oven, allow to cool and serve with crème fraîche.

Lemon Jellies with Strawberry and
Lemon Cream and Caramelised Lemon Rinds

Serves 6

For the lemon jelly:

pared rinds of 2 lemons, sliced in fine slivers
600 ml (1 pint) cold water
225 g (8 oz) granulated sugar
pared rinds of 2 lemons, cut into thicker strips than those for caramelising
300 ml (½ pint) lemon juice
5 leaves of gelatine, soaked in cold water for 10 minutes if you don't intend to
    turn the jellies out or 6 leaves if you do intend turning them out

For caramelising the lemon rinds:

300 ml (½ pint) cold water
120 g (4 oz) granulated sugar

In a small saucepan, put the fine slivers of lemon rinds into cold
water (this is not the cold water in the ingredients) and bring
to simmering point. Simmer gently for 15–20 minutes to
tenderise them. Drain through a sieve and set to one side for
caramelising later.

Pour the 600 ml (1 pint) of water into a saucepan and add
225 g (8 oz) of granulated sugar for the jellies. Add the pared
strips of lemon rind and heat the water, stirring, until every
grain of sugar has dissolved. Only when the sugar has dissolved
completely should you allow this liquid to boil and it should
boil fast and furiously for 5 minutes. Then take the saucepan off
the heat and add the lemon juice. Lemons vary so much in the
amount of juice they yield so, if squeezing the 4 lemons whose
rind you're using doesn't give the required 300 ml (½ pint),
top it up with some from a bottle of Jif Lemon Juice. Then add
the soaked gelatine, stirring until it dissolves, which will be

almost instantly. Remove the strips of lemon peel and pour the lemon liquid either into 6 large glasses if you don't intend turning them out or into 6 small moulds – I use teacups – or dariole moulds or similar if you do intend turning them out. Cover the jellies with cling film and leave them in the fridge to set, ideally overnight.

To caramelise the tenderised slivers of lemon rind, heat the 300 ml (½ pint) cold water with the 120 g (4 oz) granulated sugar (if you're having a sense of déjà vu, don't worry!) until the sugar dissolves completely. Then boil it fast for 2–3 minutes before adding the tenderised slivers of lemon rind. Poach them in this sugar syrup for 5 minutes. Then, with 2 forks, lift them from their sticky syrup onto a baking tray lined with baking parchment and leave them to cool.

For the strawberry and lemon cream:

———

300 ml (½ pint) double cream
50 g (2 oz) caster sugar
juice of 1 lemon
450 g (1 lb) perfect strawberries, hulled and crushed with a fork

———

Whip the cream and caster sugar together and then add the lemon juice. Fold the crushed strawberries through the lemon whipped cream. The whipped cream will be streaked with scarlet from the crushed berries.

If your jellies are in large glasses, divide the strawberry and lemon cream between them, spooning it on top of the jellies, and scatter a few bits of caramelised lemon rind on top of each.

Alternatively, when your lemon jellies have been turned out on their plates, spoon the strawberry and lemon cream beside them. To turn out the jellies, pour very hot water into a sink so that it is half full. Dip each container in this for several seconds, then shake out each jelly on to its plate. Garnish with the caramelised lemon rinds.

This is a perfect summer pud, with the lemon enhancing the flavour of the strawberries. The caramelised lemon rinds are optional but I do love the contrast in texture they give as a garnish.

Index